Criminal Justice
Recent Scholarship

Edited by
Marilyn McShane and Frank P. Williams III

A Series from LFB Scholarly

Search and Seizure of Digital Evidence

Robert Moore

LFB Scholarly Publishing LLC
New York 2005

Copyright © 2005 by LFB Scholarly Publishing LLC

All rights reserved.

Library of Congress Cataloging-in-Publication Data

Moore, Robert, 1976-
  Search and seizure of digital evidence / Robert Moore.
    p. cm. -- (Criminal justice)
  Includes bibliographical references and index.
  ISBN 1-59332-128-7 (alk. paper)
  1. Computer crimes--Investigation--United States. 2. Evidence, Criminal--United States. 3. Computer files--Law and legislation--United States. I. Title. II. Series: Criminal justice (LFB Scholarly Publishing LLC)
  HV8079.C65M66 2005
  345.73'0522--dc22

                                                    2005022462

ISBN 1-59332-128-7

Printed on acid-free 250-year-life paper.

Manufactured in the United States of America.

TABLE OF CONTENTS

List of Figures vii

Acknowledgements ix

Introduction xi

Chapter I: Introduction to Computer Crimes and Digital
    Evidence 1
        The Problem of Computer-Assisted Crime 9
        Purpose of This Work 13
        The Importance of Understanding Technology
        Crime and the Fourth Amendment 14

Chapter II: The High Technology Crimes and Digital
    Evidence 17
        Examining Computer Crimes 18
        Examining Cyber Crimes 33
        Past Responses to High Technology Crime 53
        Emerging Law 59
        The Volatile Nature of Digital Evidence 66
        Integrity of Digital Evidence 70

Chapter III: Search Warrants for Digital Evidence 75
        Assembling a Search Warrant Team for
        Computers 81
        Executing the Search Warrant 85

Chapter IV : Warrantless Searches and Seizures of Digital
    Evidence 97
        Warrantless Search Doctrines Applied to
        Physical Evidence 98

Application of Warrantless Search Doctrines
to the Seizure of Digital Evidence 104

Chapter V: Recommendations for the Future 143
Handling Digital Evidence 150

References 163

Appendices 179

Index 203

LIST OF FIGURES

Figure 1. A Comparison of Original File Names and Deleted File Names 67

Figure 2. An Examination of File Slack Space 68

ACKNOWLEDGEMENTS

There are so many people that contribute to any project of this magnitude. However, there are several people who have gone above and beyond in their efforts to assist me. To Dr. Stephen Mallory I express my deepest gratitude for guiding me down this path of study. To Dr. William Taylor I thank you for your assistance in organizing my thoughts and approaching this topic as I have decided to approach it. I also wish to thank Dr. Michael Smith and Dr. Lisa Nored for providing me with the skills necessary to conduct research of a legal nature and with ensuring that my reading of the court decisions was consistent with the intent of the justices and judges. Finally, I express my sincere appreciation to Ms. Linda Douglas, who helped me maintain my spirits throughout this entire process. Without each of you I would likely not have pursued this project and so I thank you for your time and efforts.

INTRODUCTION

The growth of computer-related technology has impacted almost every field of study and professional work today. In few fields has the computer revolution led to more confusion than that of the criminal justice field. As computers have become more commonplace in the lives of everyday citizens, the potential misuses for the technology have also developed. For every good use for the computer-related technology there is an equally improper use of technological devices. Many traditional crimes, as well as a few new crimes, have come to rely on computer technology. These activities have been termed computer crimes because of the use of the computer or have been referred to as cyber crimes because of the increasingly popular use of the Internet during the commission of the activities.

With the increases in technological capacity and misuses, the need has never been greater for those in the criminal justice field to gain an enhanced understanding of how computers are being improperly used. Perhaps of even greater importance, however, is for criminal justice professionals to understand the proper means of securing evidence of a computer-assisted crime. Because the evidence is more often stored on a computer, or other electronic storage medium, there may be little or no physical evidence. When it comes to determining whether or not to seize this digital evidence, it is necessary for professionals to understand exactly how the Fourth Amendment's prohibition on unreasonable searches and seizures has been adapted to account for these new forms of evidence.

To this end, the current work seeks to provide an introductory examination of how the courts have addressed such issues. In chapter one readers will be introduced to the concepts of computer crimes and cyber crimes, as well as provided information on the frequency of the problem. In chapter two readers will be introduced to several of the more commonly discussed, as well as most often encountered by professionals, crimes involving computer technology. This examination of criminal activity is designed to introduce the reader to the area of high technology crime in hopes of allowing readers to better understand the importance of properly seizing computer-related evidence. Additionally, this section will provide a brief introduction to digital evidence and how volatile the majority of evidence relating to computer-related crime may be.

Chapters three and four focus on the Fourth Amendment and its application to computer-related searches and seizures. Chapter three begins with a brief look at the issue of reasonableness of seizure, and in doing so addresses several issues associated with the drafting of a search warrant for digital evidence. Chapter four delves into the far more unstable area of warrantless search doctrines and their application to the search and seizure of computer-related evidence. In this section court decisions are examined in relation to how the courts have attempted to apply several of the warrantless search doctrines from the physical realm to the virtual world of computer-related investigations. Chapter five recounts the major results of the work as well as providing a foundation for future study as this area of search and seizure law is certain to continue changing in the coming years.

It is in fact the very nature of computer technology that these doctrines will change. To see how rapid change is in relationship to computer technology, one should only think back to only ten years ago and then consider how

Introduction

developed computers and the Internet have become in this time frame. Another problem with studying this area of jurisprudence is that very few of these doctrines have been directly applied to computer-related investigations by the United State Supreme Court. As a result there are several doctrines that have been applied differently from state to state and circuit to circuit. And finally there is the problem of rapidly changing court decisions. Every effort has been made to ensure that the current work contains the most up-to-date cases and legal analysis. Unfortunately the rapid changes in this area mean that it is possible that during the publication process one or more of these doctrines may be modified or nullified by the courts. Interested readers should use the current work as a starting point for conducting their own research into this incredibly interesting and extremely demanding area of study.

CHAPTER I

Introduction to Computer Crimes and Digital Evidence

In recent years society has witnessed a remarkable increase in both the quality and quantity of technology available. Few individuals would dispute that new technologies have made life easier; however, there is also little disputing that these same advantages of technology are accompanied by disadvantages. Among the disadvantages is the misuse of technology. Today it appears as though as fast as new technology is developed a misuse for the technology is discovered. According to Dearne (2001), 85% of all United States businesses reported their computer or network security are breached every year, with many of these breaches having resulted in significant financial losses for the victims. Many victim corporations have been unable to quantify their losses; but for those who have been able to assign a value to the losses, the total appears to be greater than $700 million each year. The two most common computer-based attacks against corporations are theft of proprietary information and fraud, with the Internet being the most common means of entry (Dearne, 2001).

The development of these misuses has required the development of new terminology, as well as reclassifications of criminal activity in light of technology. Crimes involving technology are now often labeled as either "cyber crime" or "computer crime". Casey (2000) defines cyber crime as any criminal offense in which computers and networks are used either as the targets or as instruments of the crime, while defining computer crime as any crime in which a computer is used and the use of the computer is enumerated in the statute.

As noted by Casey's definition, there have been traditional attempts to fully distinguish between computer crimes and cyber crimes. In 2000, for example, Meinel defined computer crime as illegal acts directly involving a computer - such as computer theft or hacking, which is the unauthorized access of another's computer system. Casey's (2000) definition of cyber crime related to illegal acts that might or might not involve a computer; with the outstanding example being the crime of stalking, where an individual may stalk a victim in the physical world, the virtual world of the Internet or both. Recently, however, statute law has tended to consolidate computer crime and cyber crime, narrowing the definition to those criminal offenses involving the use of a computer in the commission of an illegal act.

Perhaps a continued distinction between the two would be beneficial to those who are not actively involved in investigating or researching these areas of criminal activity. By relying on Casey's (2000) definition of cyber crime an individual who is investigating a cyber crime would need to be aware that the crime could involve acts in the physical realm that do not involve a computer or a network. However, increased awareness of crimes involving technology have likely even removed the need for this distinction, as any crime that involves a computer or a network will still maintain some level of physical realm involvement

Statutory simplification has of course presented problems for those involved in the investigation and research of crimes involving technology. Currently, there are two ways of coping with the problem. First, some merely refer to all of the crimes as cyber crimes, thereby removing the existence of the computer crime. This can be evidenced by the number of books currently scheduled for release in the next few years involving the term cyber crime in the title. Each of these books discusses both computer crimes and cyber crimes, yet makes no mention of computers in the title. Second, the two crimes are being grouped under a general heading that has come to be known as "high technology crime". High technology crime or "high tech crime" as it is sometimes referred to as has been defined by Coutorie (1995) as crime involving the use of any form of sophisticated electronic device such as a computer, cellular telephone, or other digital means of communication that is in common use today. The term "sophisticated technology" is used to distinguish between technology such as firearms, which are technological devices, and technology such as personal data assistants or telephones, which are highly developed electronic devices.

There are many high technology crimes that could be considered both physically and financially dangerous; however, those most encountered by law enforcement include hacking, phone phreaking, child pornography and identity theft. Hacking, which is also commonly referred to as "cracking", refers to the act of gaining unauthorized access to software programs or other computers through a combination of computer programming and password cracking skills (Casey, 2000; Meinel, 2000). Because of the level of reliance placed on computers today, this is potentially one of the more dangerous types of high technology crime. For example, one need only examine the many components of our nation's critical infrastructure that is dependent upon computers. One of the more common examples here would be the operation of one of the dams around the United States. Imagine the damage that could be inflicted upon a community if the floodgates to one of these dams could be opened by a hacker. Thankfully, this is currently considered almost impossible. Yet, the truth is that any computer is a vulnerable computer. Even removing all of these computers from the various networks would not completely remove the risks. This process, sometimes referred to as land locking a computer, would not prevent the computer from being hacked via access from within the facility. In this example the hacker could have penetrated the system from either the network or from within the facility. It is for this reason that discussions on computer security do not rely purely on high technical jargon. Basic commonsense computer security is also necessary to protect technological assets.

Telecommunications fraud is the second high tech crime considered. Perpetrators of these types of crimes often refer to themselves as "phreakers", with the term phreaker being used to describe individuals who have devoted a significant portion of their lives to understanding how phone systems operate and then use this understanding to commit crimes through the use of the telephone system. Perhaps the best example of this crime involves the escapades of Kevin Poulsen. Poulsen once rerouted telephone calls into a local radio station in an effort to win a car. By rerouting the calls to the station, Poulsen was assured of being the 227th caller and winning a Porsche (Littman, 1997). Because these crimes may pose a slight physical danger to society, many consider these crimes non-dangerous. However, these crimes are extremely dangerous and maintain the potential for a disastrous financial effect. In the year 2000, North America lost $500 billion in telecommunications revenue (Royal Canadian

Mounted Police, 2001). Financial loses in turn translate into higher phone service fees for private citizens as the phone companies are forced to recover their losses in some manner.

Identity theft is the third high tech crime warranting increased understanding by individuals in the criminal justice field. This term is sometimes misunderstood because there are actually two different types of identity theft. First, there is physical identity theft, which is the lesser-known form of identity theft and refers to the process by which an individual will assume another's physical identity. Normally this assumption of identity is used to either commit a crime or escape from something in the identity thief's past. This form of high tech crime has the most potential to be abused by individuals who engage in business activities with organized crime groups. The ability to steal someone's identity is something crime figures could use to hide themselves during periods of intense scrutiny following high profile criminal activity. The second area of identity theft is actually more akin to credit fraud. Here, an individual who has managed to steal personal information belonging to the victim assumes that person's credit life and proceeds to destroy the individual's credit record by going on shopping sprees and opening new accounts (Newman, 1999). Much like telecommunications fraud, this form of identity theft poses a financial threat to society because credit card companies will attempt to recover their losses through increased rates for legitimate users.

The fourth and final high technology crime considered is that of child pornography, or "digital child pornography", as it is commonly referred to when the crime involves images or videos being transmitted via the Internet. The vast increase in computer technology has resulted in increasing numbers of child pornography violators. This particular crime could be considered one of the most, if not the most, dangerous crime because the activity involves the sexual abuse of children. Also, the increased technological capacity has resulted in a frightening increase in the frequency of this crime.

It is worth noting that there are many additional crimes other than those just discussed. For example, there is the illegal use of steganography, which is hidden writing (Johnson, 2000); encryption, which is the scrambling of information and has recently received coverage in the debate over expectations of privacy and the rights of the government (Diffie & Landau, 1998; Edgett, 2003); embezzlement or theft of funds (Rush, 2000); which can sometimes fall under hacking (Judson, 1994); theft of bandwidth, which refers to the process of stealing Internet speed (Meinel, 2000); and intellectual property theft (Paradise, 1999; Lee, 1997), which refers to the process of trading copyrighted music, videos or pictures via the Internet. Despite the vast number of aforementioned crimes, most books and reports issued by Federal agencies that handle the investigation of technology assisted crime, or reports that deal with the frequency of these crimes, discuss the four crimes listed in the text above. Put simply, hacking, phreaking, child pornography and identity theft are the more high profile cases and are the ones more likely to be encountered for now.

Although awareness of high technology crimes is increasing, such crimes still present many problems for the criminal justice system both in the United States and abroad. When searching for evidence of the worldwide implications of high technology crime one has to look no further than the case involving the Love Bug virus. The virus was part of an illegal thesis, written and programmed by a student at a university in the Philippines. The thesis was initially designed to steal Internet passwords, but the Love Bug virus expanded the original programming. Not only did the program steal Internet passwords, but it also damaged the computer systems from which the passwords were removed. According to Antionline (2000), several companies placed their losses at as much as $10 billion when combining the damage to equipment with the lost time and payroll necessary to correct the problems created by the virus.

Many of the companies affected were both shocked and outraged when the charges against the student were dropped. Why were the charges dropped? There was no lack of desire to prosecute the individual. The prosecution, however, lacked a statute criminalizing the student's actions. The Philippines, at that time, had no statutes relating to computer hacking or the criminal misuse of computers. The statutes under which the prosecution first attempted to charge the student required evidence they could not obtain. Since the release of the Love Bug Virus, the legislature in the Philippines has worked to increase its knowledge of laws relating to high technology crimes, and today an act such as the student's would be prosecutable (Brenner & Koops, 2004).

Here in the United States it is becoming increasingly important for professionals involved in the day to day operations of the criminal justice system to gain a better understanding of computer-related crime and electronic evidence. Court personnel, as well as law enforcement professionals, have a need to understand that computers may be involved in criminal activity as either a primary means of committing the act, as is the case of computer-assisted crime, or as a repository of evidence related to a criminal activity, as is the case with crimes such as narcotics trafficking (Baron-Evans & Murphy, 2003). More troubling than the aforementioned examples is the fact that perhaps as much as 75% of computer related crimes go unreported. Victims of technology crime, individuals and corporations alike, have indicated a lack of desire to report technology crimes, believing that the police will not be able to handle the investigation (Clark & Diliberto, 1996). Such an opinion may have once been justified. Only a decade ago, when computer crime was just beginning to account for a larger number or overall crimes, and its danger was still in the infant phase, many United States justice agencies expressed a lack of concern for computer crime. Donn B. Parker, one of the foremost computer security advisers in the country, once wrote that he did not believe viruses and other computer hacking tricks would amount to much (Denning, 1990; Parker, 1976). In fact, he criticized agencies for their efforts to increase awareness of the technology crime problem. It was Parker's opinion that the harmful effects that could potentially be caused by future computer criminals were not as serious as sources initially indicated. He believed the problem did not justify the extensive, and sometimes expensive, research that was being put into preparations for future computer crimes (Denning, 1990). This is sad proof that technology crimes were not taken seriously when it was still possible to form adequate protections, protections that could have potentially limited several of the more damaging attacks that have occurred in recent years. Thankfully, there are few today who feel this way, including Parker.

Society is now facing an era when all areas of the criminal justice system are being forced to consider high technology crimes. Today, many criminal justice agencies are beginning to reconsider whether technology crime units could be helpful in their departments. In fact, many are going even further and beginning to examine whether these units may actually be necessary. For these reasons, it is going to become increasingly necessary to reevaluate the need for technology crime units that are adequately trained to handle related investigations.

The Problem of Computer-Assisted Crime

Individuals who would misuse new technology are constantly improving their techniques, as evidenced by the increasing number of websites and chat rooms that allow individuals to discuss methods of applying technology to criminal activities. Today, all one has to do to locate these chat rooms is spend time on the Internet. While some of the truly informative websites may be difficult to locate, time spent weeding through the false links and useless sites will ultimately result in a useful website.

Another problem relates to how to conduct investigations of crimes that can take place anywhere in the world. As evidenced by the earlier example of the Love Bug virus, computer criminals can come from anywhere around the world. As law enforcement agencies begin to implement responses plans to counter these problems, the issue of jurisdiction is certain to become a consideration. Jurisdiction not only impacts international investigations but also investigations involving multiple states. Brenner and Koops (2004) have proposed that the answer to this will eventually involve jurisdiction determined on the basis of where the crime's effects are witnessed rather than where the crime originated. Unfortunately, the current state of technology crime investigations is still too young to speculate exactly how well this approach can be applied.

In examining the issue of investigative teams here in the United States, past attempts have disclosed that only 1 out of every 15 law enforcement agencies had any information relating to technology crimes. Criminal justice agencies must accept the fact that changes must be made if law enforcement is to keep pace with the individuals who would seek to misuse society's greatest technologies. The events of September 11, 2001 have resulted in numerous restructuring changes among federal law enforcement agencies. As more of these federal agencies find their resources redirected toward investigations involving matters of national security, fewer resources will be available to handle technology-assisted crimes. The current trend in some federal agencies is to focus on the use of computers in terrorist activities. It is only reasonable to believe that within a few years investigations involving high tech crimes will be handled by state and local law enforcement agencies, or there will be no investigations conducted. It is when these initial concerns are addressed that the more complex issues such as jurisdiction may be finalized.

The lack of trained law enforcement investigators to handle technology crime investigations has resulted in the proliferation of "cyber private eyes". These are individuals or companies that handle computer forensic investigations the government either will not or cannot investigate. Often, individuals and corporations who do not wish to make public their problem will turn to these agencies (Wang, 2001). If the criminal justice field is to match the skill level of high tech criminals, then more law enforcement officers must undergo training that will allow them to become familiar with not only the technology but also the history and methodology of current high technology crimes.

Introduction to Computer Crimes and Digital Evidence

Today, there are more books available on high technology crimes than ever before, but many have little to offer the field of criminal justice. Part of this problem lies in the stylistic writings of these works; a majority of the literature is written from a highly technical standpoint. These types of technical manuals may be necessary for someone who is going to work in the information technology field, or even for someone who is considering a career in computer forensics, but they are of little use to most law enforcement officers. Another problem with the current literature is a lack of coverage of important legal issues associated with the investigation of high technology crimes. Investigations involving high technology crimes are not like many other investigations, and as such require that investigating officers be equipped with knowledge of the legal issues surrounding an investigation. Failure to provide investigators with information on the legal ramifications of search and seizure in cases involving technological devices could result in the evidence being dismissed from trial. Failure to properly secure digital evidence, which is defined as evidence stored on magnetic media such as a computer hard disk or CD-ROM, may be equivalent to never obtaining the evidence. If the seizure of the evidence is not handled properly the first time then it may be destroyed or lost to the prosecution.

It is for these reasons that it is important for individuals employed in the field of criminal justice to have more than a cursory understanding of how the Fourth Amendment has been applied to the handling of digital evidence and high technology crime investigations. The Fourth Amendment is one of the more legally complex components of American due process, and it is even more complex when the issues are framed in the context of digital evidence and cyberspace – the infinite online world that exists when one accesses the Internet. Many of the judicial interpretations of the Fourth Amendment in the physical realm are at most marginally applicable to searches involving technological devices and digital evidence.

Indeed, a review of relevant case law leads one to question whether the Fourth Amendment can even be applied to issues involving technology; and, even if the courts are to begin interpreting Fourth Amendment jurisprudence in light of technology, there is still the technology lag to consider. An appeal making its way through the courts may take anywhere from one year to three years. During this time, it is possible, even likely, that technology could evolve to the point where a judicial holding is irrelevant. Perhaps the greatest example of this is the case of Napster, which was a program designed to allow users to swap music files via the Internet. When owners of the intellectual property rights discovered this was happening they immediately filed suit against the company for allowing the trade of copyrighted materials to pass through their servers. By the time a court ruled on the software, subsequent companies to release similar file-trading programs had developed a means of circumventing the ruling.

As a result of rulings such as this there are some who debate whether it is time for Congress and not the courts to step in and modify the rules of criminal procedure to account for technology. Kerr (2005) argues that Congress may be the solution to developing solid rules that do not vary from jurisdiction to jurisdiction. However, on the other side of this issue are others who argue that the solution does not rely on new procedures but merely an adherence to previously established criminal procedure. For these individuals the answer is not in modifying the Fourth Amendment because of technology, but rather in making technology adhere to the Fourth Amendment standards generated in the physical realm (Ziff, 2005).

Purpose of This Work

The purpose of this work is to provide information about the problems associated with the application of traditional search-and-seizure jurisprudence to cases involving high technology crimes. In line with Kerr's (2005) arguments, this author feels there are many problems with applying the Fourth Amendment doctrines to searches and seizures involving technology. In an attempt to provide a better understanding of why the Fourth Amendment is so important to investigations of high technology crimes, the four high technology crimes most frequently encountered by law enforcement personnel are defined, discussed in both a historical and a contemporary context. The author has attempted to simplify complex technological information, thereby making it useful to both academics and law enforcement professionals who encounter these criminal activities.

The Fourth Amendment's regulation of search and seizure will certainly emerge as one of the more important and most debated areas of jurisprudence as the courts begin to examine technology and its use in criminal activity. This conclusion is based on the fact that few high technology crimes leave significant amounts of physical evidence; the majority of the evidence left is digital in nature and stored on a technological device. An investigator's decision to search a computer system with or without a warrant can significantly impact a high technology crime investigation.

The federal courts have only recently begun to examine this area of law, and because there have been few rulings by the Supreme Court, the lower courts have been forced to examine these issues themselves, often with differing opinions on key issues. This work examines several of these lower-court holdings in an attempt to point out the dangers and difficulties of applying the Fourth Amendment to investigations of technology-assisted crimes. The various decisions are synthesized, thereby providing a resource for individuals who desire to develop and implement standard operating procedures concerning the seizure of technological devices and digital evidence.

Along with the various legal issues associated with decisions regarding search and seizure, this work also provides a basic understanding of several issues associated with the preparation and execution of a search warrant on a digital crime scene. Recently, there have been several publications on the subject. While these documents are good resources for investigators, there is no one guide that provides a detailed analysis of the procedures. Thus, this work seeks to provide a more accurate presentation of the issues associated with the execution of search warrants for high technology crime scenes.

The Importance of Understanding Technology Crime and the Fourth Amendment

Currently, very few state and local law enforcement agencies in the United States are active in the investigation of high technology crimes. Although there is hope as more agencies are investigating high technology crime today than they were five years ago, there are still many agencies that do not maintain personnel and resources to handle such crimes. There are many different reasons that could explain such a low number of investigative units. One argument involves the theory that law enforcement agencies are not technically prepared to investigate these crimes. The equipment necessary for conducting high technology crime investigations can be extremely expensive, especially when the costs of training are factored into the equation. Further, there is the issue of locating individuals who are capable and willing to investigate technology-assisted crime. Individuals in academia who play a role in the education and training of tomorrow's criminal justice leaders could assist in this endeavor by providing a greater understanding of the importance and necessity of high technology crime investigations.

A survey conducted by the Mississippi Statistical Analysis Center (2002), a research unit associated with The University of Southern Mississippi's Department of Justice Administration, revealed that over one-half of Mississippi law enforcement agencies believed high tech crimes were on the rise, with a majority of these agencies desiring more training in the field. This problem and needs assessment, however, is not unique to the State of Mississippi.

These results, while the study only focused on Mississippi, should not be limited to this one state. In recent years there has been a national push for increased awareness of the problem of high technology crime. Proof of this can be found in the fact that more technology professionals and software designers are offering both forensic software programs and hands-on training for law enforcement officers and others in the criminal justice field. The issue of search and seizure, however, has received little or no coverage in the curricula of these programs. As the problem of high technology crime continues to increase, agencies that can develop high technology crime units will place itself at the forefront of the field. With the aforementioned statement in mind, it is this author's hope that this work and its coverage of the issues surrounding the

Fourth Amendment will serve as a resource for agencies and individuals that are currently undertaking just such an endeavor.

CHAPTER II

The High Technology Crimes and Digital Evidence

Hacking is one of the more highly publicized high technology crimes, but it is not the most physically threatening. Incidents of hacking will generally result in financial losses, but there are crimes like the transmission of child pornography and cyber stalking that can lead to more physically destructive criminal acts. Freeh (2002) has stated his belief that the vast majority of individuals who possess child pornography do so with the intent of using the materials to one day groom a child for possible sexual relations with the perpetrator. Freeh, a former director of the Federal Bureau of Investigation, made his statement on the basis of the investigations he and the agency handled during his tenure. Regardless of whether one decides to accept Freeh's belief, there is little denying that child pornography is a dangerous crime that leads to physical and emotional harm for the child victims who are forced to pose for the images and videos.

Historically, many in the criminal justice field have been loathe to commit scarce resources to high technology crimes, and have displayed little desire to conduct investigations involving computers and technology. Further, these same law enforcement officers may have felt high technology crime was not a problem in their jurisdiction. The truth is that more traditionally physical crimes are being aided by technology every day, and almost every jurisdiction will eventually encounter technology-assisted crime. Proof of this is provided by recent reports regarding current trends in narcotics trafficking. Recent studies of the activities of drug traffickers have shown an increase in their reliance on the Internet and e-mail (Krane, 2002). Due to the fact that e-mail can be difficult to trace if law enforcement officers are not adequately trained, drug traffickers will eventually find a use for the technology. Absent the use of the computer as a means of communication, another scenario is the drug trafficker who uses his or her computer to keep records of transactions. Should an officer encounter an individual who is using a computer to commit a crime such as narcotics trafficking, an understanding of procedural and technical issues may allow for the recovery of evidence that otherwise would be lost.

Examining Computer Crimes

For the purpose of this work, Casey's (2000) definition of computer crime will be used. Under this definition, a crime is considered a computer crime if the activity involves a computer and the statute criminalizing the activity makes specific mention of the use of computers. When examining computer crimes under this definition the computer may be involved in the crime in one of three ways. First, the computer may be an instrument of the crime, meaning that the computer was required to commit the crime. Second, the computer may be the fruit of the crime, which means that a criminal activity involves the theft or damage of a computer. Finally, the computer may be a repository of evidence, such as when evidence of criminal activity is stored on the computer. Perhaps the two most common and financially devastating types of computer crimes are hacking, which is also sometimes referred to as cracking and involves the illegal accessing of another's computer (Meinel, 2000), and phreaking, which is abuse of the telecommunications system (Wang, 2001). Both of the aforementioned crimes can be called computer crimes because they are made illegal through statutes such as 18 U.S.C. 1030, the Computer Fraud and Abuse Act, which makes unapproved access to another's computer a crime.

Hacking and Cracking

Many erroneously associate the term "hacking" with the image of a small, fragile, nerdy-looking teenager sitting in front of his computer. There are several potentially valid reasons for this misconception. When computers were first released, those who could be considered among the intellectual elite purchased the majority of units; and these individuals were commonly referred to as computer nerds. These individuals would spend hours every day working on their machines (Levy, 1994). It was this addiction by many of these individuals that likely contributed to this misconception. However, Hollywood also contributed to the problem. There have been several films that have only strengthened the belief that a nerd and his computer work together to create mischief. Individuals who are not familiar with a true hacker may base their opinions on what they have seen on television or in movies. For example, movies such as **Hackers** and **Wargames** seem to be the basis for many people's understanding of the types of activities to be expected from a hacker. Another consideration is that older and experienced hackers are not as careless as their younger counterparts who make news headlines with their criminal activities (Power, 2000).

It is important to note that a hacker today is not the same thing as what a hacker was when the term was coined.

Many original hackers believe that computer security is important and will use their skills, which may or may not have been developed through the commission of illegal acts and past security exploits, to help others prepare their computer systems for defense against the same security exploits they may have once abused themselves (Wilson, 2001). If one examines the vast number of websites maintained on the World Wide Web that discuss hacking and exploits, it could be postulated that these individuals were influenced by the Hollywood stereotype of hackers and not the security-conscious individuals. These individuals appear to have convinced themselves and others that by taking over websites or writing some new form of computer virus they are making themselves more recognized or revered by others in the hacker community. Despite the fact that hackers today are not the same as the hackers of the 1960s and 1970s, it is still important to understand both what a hacker was in the beginning and what a hacker is today. To facilitate this understanding a brief history on the evolution of computer hacking and cracking warrants discussion.

The founders and original team members of the Artificial Intelligence Lab at the Massachusetts Institute of Technology (MIT) (Levy, 1994) originated the term hacker. These individuals were not computer criminals but instead a group of dedicated researchers who could exploit computer programs to accomplish tasks for which they were not originally designed. They called themselves hackers because of their ability to spend hours hacking away on the keyboard. Levy (1994) acknowledges this origin, but also notes that the term's origin may have come much earlier. Based on interviews with several students of MIT, Levy believes the term "hack" was originally associated with the elaborate pranks committed among faculty and students as early as the 1950s. The students from whom Levy received his information claimed the term was used to describe any action that was imbued with creativity, extreme style and technical virtue.

That MIT was the source of original hackers should not come as a great surprise. MIT was one of the first universities to offer computer-programming classes, so it seems only natural that the first university to offer courses on an invention as incredible as the computer would also be the location of the earliest development of a computer-related culture. It should be noted that these individuals were not criminals in the sense that they broke state or federal laws. These so-called hackers did, however, violate several school policies when they became so obsessed with not only achieving competency on the computer, but also with gaining complete mastery over the device. It has even been stated by some that the computer industry owes its development to many of these early hackers because several went on to become leaders in the movement to establish computers as an integral part of society (Levy, 1994). These individuals were not, however, completely devoted to businesslike developments of computers and their beneficial use to small businesses and personal users. For example, the original computer programmers from MIT are credited with the development of several useful computer applications, but they are also credited with the development of the first video games (Levy, 1994).

The term hacker was not associated with criminal activity until computer-assisted crime began to gain more publicity. At this time, the media applied the term hacker to the individuals who were gaining unauthorized access to other individuals' computers. The original coiners of the term hacker immediately expressed, and still do, the opinion that the term for those breaking into computers without permission should be "crackers", or criminal hackers (Denning, 1990). Today, however, the term hacker has become so linked to computer crime that it would be almost impossible to separate the two.

Occasionally the term cracker is used when someone is discussing computer-assisted crime, but the term does not refer to a hacker as the original hackers requested. Computer professionals now refer to someone as a cracker if they are responsible for cracking passwords, software protections or copyright protections on digital videodiscs or software programs (Casey, 2000). It should be understood that if an individual hears the terms hacker and cracker when they are examining computers and crime, more than likely the originator of the discussion is referring to the hacker as the one who breaks into the computer and the cracker is the one who is cracking passwords. Unfortunately the terms have become so ingrained that it is unlikely that the original hackers of MIT will ever be able to separate the two terms.

The issue, as well as the threat, of computer crime existed long before technology evolved to a point where two computers could link up to exchange information (Bequai, 1978; Bequai, 1987). It was, however, this initial linking of computers that provided the foundation for what would ultimately lead society to a point where computer hacking now poses a threat against not only national but also international infrastructure security. One of the greatest impacts on computer hacking came from the introduction of the ARPANET, or what would today be called the Internet. ARPANET, which stands for Advanced Research Projects Agency Network, was launched in 1969 when researchers linked four computers to share information and computer resources between the various facilities. It is interesting to note that the original researchers responsible for the ARPANET indicated when they first launched this network that they believed the idea would alter the natural way of life for individuals (Denning, 1990). There is little denying that the Internet has influenced almost every life today. Ironically, the technology originally intended to be a tool for research and development has become one of the most used criminal tools in history.

Hacking was around in the 1970's, beginning almost immediately after the initial launching of the ARPANET, but it was not until the 1980's that the public truly began to take notice of the problem. Prior to the 80's, few people even took the time to understand what was involved in the act of hacking. Computers were so foreign to most individuals that many did not understand the benefits of the devices, and as such cared even less about the potential dangers involved. One of the events that sparked a change in this perception came in mid-1983, when a series of serious computer break-ins occurred. The computer break-ins compromised 60 or more computers, with the targets ranging from the Memorial Sloan-Kettering Cancer Center to the Los Alamos National Laboratory (Trigaux, 2000).

An FBI probe was immediately launched, and the investigation led to the discovery of a teenage gang of computer hackers known as the 414 Gang. The club, which derived its name from the area code in which its members lived and committed their crimes, was eventually charged with the break-ins. This series of computer break-ins shocked the American people, with many immediately demanding better protection from high tech hoodlums (Denning, 1990). It is interesting that the public immediately assumed that all computer criminals were juveniles. Perhaps this is attributable to the fact that few adults saw much need for personal computers beyond that of playing video games, an act normally associated with juveniles. Further, the fact that all of the 414 Gang were juveniles likely influenced the public's perception of the crime. The truth was more likely the same then as it is today. There are as many or more adults engaged in hacking as there are kids engaged in the act.

The next major incident to spark the public's interest in the crime of hacking occurred on November 2, 1988, when Robert Morris, a Cornell University graduate student in the computer science department, released a computer worm program from a MIT computer lab. A worm program is not unlike a virus in that the worm program will usually complete a function and then replicate itself repeatedly and resent itself back out over the Internet. This constant duplication and remailing can slow down a network to the point of collapse, as was the case of Robert Morris' worm program. Morris' graduate emphasis was in computer security, and when he wrote the worm program it was his intent to develop a program to use as practice for examining computer security. The program was designed to copy itself onto each computer in the MIT lab and then hide itself until he could remove the program. Unfortunately, an error in programming caused the worm to replicate at an unforeseeable rate. The program then took advantage of the various computers connected to the network at the university and copied itself onto 2000 or 3000 computers by jumping across the Internet. This rapid copying caused the affected computers to run out of memory and shut down completely (Denning, 1990; Hafner & Markoff, 1991).

On November 7, 1988, the FBI became involved with the Morris case. Once Morris was located, there was some debate concerning what charges should be filed against him, as he did not intend to let the worm program run free (Hafner & Markoff, 1991). Through careful analysis of the

Computer Fraud and Abuse Act of 1986, the FBI was able to prosecute Morris. Morris's computer program, and the subsequent events that led to his arrest and prosecution, resulted in Robert Morris being inducted into several hacker halls of fame. It is unclear whether it has been determined that Morris received such notoriety because he was a true hacker or merely because his arrest and trial made him one of, if not the first, individuals charged under the newly established Computer Fraud and Abuse Act.

Due to the unique circumstances surrounding Morris' case, the Cornell Commission was formed and charged with the duty of investigating the incident and making recommendations for preventing future occurrences. The Commission acknowledged that Morris's actions had revealed a serious defect in the computer systems used in the various agencies, and conceded that the events and evidence did show that the systems needed reevaluation; however, the Commission still maintained that Morris should neither be released nor have his punishment reduced (Denning, 1990). The Commission also examined The Computer Fraud and Abuse Act of 1986, and determined that the government merely had to provide proof that Morris intentionally and without authorization accessed federal computers. It was the Commission's belief that during the course of the trial the prosecution was in fact able to prove that Morris intentionally accessed the computers because he knowingly took advantage of several holes in the UNIX operating system (Hafner & Markoff, 1991). Therefore, despite the fact that Morris did not intend to let his program loose, he was convicted on January 22, 1990, sentenced to three years probation, fined $10,000, and ordered to perform 400 hours of community service (Denning, 1990).

The case of Robert Morris and that of the 414 Gang are examples of early hacking cases that began the process of the media covering computer crimes. The problem is that both of these cases involved only limited media coverage. For example, the 414 Gang's crimes brought attention to the citizens of Minnesota and a few surrounding states, but the nation was still generally unaware of what was happening. It would, however, be only a few more years after the case of Robert Morris before the entire nation would become aware of the power a hacker could wield and the publicity one could generate. Throughout the late 1980s and 1990s, citizens on a small and local level began to take notice of the stories concerning Kevin Mitnick. Mitnick would eventually become known as one of the most, if not the most, infamous computer hackers in the world (Gill, 2001). In the 1990s, Mitnick gained great notoriety when a computer engineer, Tatsuo Shimomura, tracked him cross-country. This engineer became interested in the case when Mitnick illegally accessed his computer for information on a cellular phone project on which he was working (Littman, 1996). The case began a nationwide manhunt. Mitnick's reputation grew to the point that he was the first computer criminal to be featured on the television show America's Most Wanted, and a book entitled *Takedown* has been written chronicling his chase (Penenberg, 1999). The movie **Hackers II** is also a chronicle of the events that led to Mitnick's invasion of Shimomura's computer and the subsequent cross-country chase.

Mitnick is perhaps responsible, or at the very least one of the forerunners responsible, for scaring the government into believing that computer hacking could be dangerous. When Mitnick was finally captured and charged, his sentence was more severe than many manslaughter sentences at the time. This is despite the fact that Mitnick never used, copied or damaged any information that he accessed prior to his going on the run (Kornblum, 1997). Instead, Mitnick claimed he was just challenging himself, which incidentally was his reasoning for many criminal acts over the course of his career. By combining his skills in computer hacking and impersonation with his desire to challenge himself, Mitnick managed to gain access to some of the most guarded computer systems in the country (Hafner & Markoff, 1991).

Mitnick's reputation for manipulating technological devices was so great that prison administrators feared what he could do if he got his hands on a computer. There are two good examples provided by Penenberg (1999) that present evidence of the administration's fear. The first incident occurred when Mitnick was placed in solitary confinement after prison officials were informed he was attempting to turn his Walkman radio into a bugging device. According to the informant, Mitnick was planning to place the bug in the warden's office. The second incident involved Mitnick being denied access to unsupervised phone calls because prison administrators were afraid he could dial into the computers of the United States Department of Defense, which Mitnick reportedly did several times over the course of his career. It is worth noting that Mitnick himself has never confirmed this information (Penenberg, 1999).

Currently, the level of technology used in the commission of hacking crimes is greater than ever before, but there is a positive side to this issue. When most of these earlier examples occurred, there were few good computer crime statutes in place. Today, this is not true. There are now federal statutes, as well as many individual state criminal statutes, that provide punishment for those who would misuse computers or illegally access others' computers. Further, Congress has recently considered the role of computers in possible terrorist activity. The original draft of the act known as the Anti-Terrorism Act (ATA) made hacking a crime of terrorism because of the potential for damage to United States computers by agencies of other governments. Under the ATA, a conviction for hacking that involved any federal computer would result in the individual receiving life imprisonment without the possibility of parole. The USA PATRIOT Act has been passed in place of the Anti-Terrorism Act, and it remains to be seen how this act will affect the future of other computer crime statutes that may have been considered.

The Crime of Phreaking

The crime of phreaking is often represented as the oldest of computer crimes because phone phreaking, even though it was not known as phreaking at the time, occurred in 1870. The crime was committed when a group of teenagers tapped into the phone lines and redirected outgoing phone calls. These individuals were caught and restricted from using the newly established phone system. All of this occurred shortly after the phone system was first made available (Trigaux, 2000).

Phreaking is still common today, but it is not as well known as computer hacking. Part of the problem could lie in the fact that few media reports or movies have been made that attempt to glamorize phreaking in the same manner as the crime of hacking. This should not be construed as a statement concerning any trend in the commission of this crime, as the crime is still commonly encountered today. For example, when individuals receive their phone bills at the end of the month and complain about long-distance charges they did not make, then these individuals are potential victims of phone phreakers. It should be noted that when examining the aforementioned description of phreaking, the term phreak is intentionally misspelled with a "ph" in place of an "f". This change in spelling is used by perpetrators of phone phreaking activities out of appreciation for the device that provides them with their entertainment - the telephone (Wang, 2001).

The crime of phreaking has been around since the development of the phone system in the late 1800s, but it appears that the one incident in 1870 was an isolated event. Over the last century, there surely have been small instances of phone phreaking occurring, but it was not until the 1970's that the practice began to gain notoriety and popularity. It is believed that a 1971 article in *Esquire* magazine must be considered the turning point in the popularity of phone phreaking. In the article an unnamed blind boy was reportedly able to make free phone calls by mimicking the sounds of the phone system using nothing but his lips. This young man had told several other blind friends about the trick, and before long there were several blind children attempting to learn about the phone system, how the system worked and how various tones could impact the control of the phone system (Draper, 2001).

One of these young men was a friend of John Draper, an engineering student. Draper became interested in the telephone system and eventually developed an almost unquenchable thirst for information relating to how the telephone worked. Along with another friend, Draper began an in-depth examination of the telephone system (D.K., 1996). Draper would earn the nickname Capt'n Crunch in the 1960s when he was able to repeatedly make free phone calls using nothing more than a whistle he had obtained from a box of cereal. By blowing a precise tone into the earpiece of the telephone, Draper was able to open the phone lines and direct them however he saw fit (D.K., 1996). This ability so greatly motivated Draper and his blind friend that they began to spend large amounts of time each day learning about the specifics of telephone communications. Draper's blind friend eventually became good enough that he could whistle the sounds required to trick the telephone system and open the phone lines to make calls.

Draper was also the first to develop an electronic blue box. This device mimicked the electronic tones emitted to control telephone lines. Draper named the boxes blue boxes because the original casings for his work were blue boxes obtained from Radio Shack. Eventually the phone companies became aware of Draper's actions and after repeated warnings both Draper and his friend were formerly charged. The two became instant media celebrities because of their arrest (Draper, 2001).

Draper and his friend were among the first phone phreakers to develop their talents, but the true impact of these individuals lies in the individuals they influenced. Draper's escapades influenced several up-and-coming phone phreakers, two of the more notorious of which are Steve Jobs and Kevin Poulsen. Both of these individuals would eventually become known for their influence on the computer industry and the hacking culture, but they both also began their careers as phone phreaks, a term used to identify these individuals who were interested in telecommunications. Before Steve Jobs started Apple Computers, he made his living in college by selling blue boxes based on the designs provided by Draper. Because the blue boxes allowed the user to trick the phone line into opening a free connection, the device became popular among college students who could call friends and family at anytime for no charge (Nesteroff, 1997).

Unlike Steve Jobs, who played with phone phreaking before moving on to a professional career in the computer industry, Kevin Poulsen spent the entire early part of his life in and out of trouble for phone phreaking. Beginning at the age of thirteen, he used the braces his parents purchased for him as a means of gaining access to the telephone system. According to Littman (1997), Poulsen's early obsession with the phone system was one of curiosity. Kevin would entertain himself and his friends by going to a mall and using one of the pay phones to make a prank phone call in which he would jump through several phone exchanges before ringing the phone located directly next to him (Littman, 1997).

As Poulsen got older, his phone exploits continued to get more outrageous. At one point in his life, Poulsen was routinely breaking into the main headquarters of a local telephone company in an attempt to gain access to manuals and training documentation that later provided him with invaluable insight into how the company's main computer, the controller for the entire telephone system, worked. With access to this computer, Poulsen was able to develop his skills to the level that he could tap into anyone's telephone line. According to Littman (1997) this ability resulted in several of Kevin's friends refusing to even talk on their phones after he informed two buddies that he had overheard a conversation in which they laughed at how obsessed he was with telephones.

Eventually Poulsen was arrested for his abuse of the telephone system. Before his capture, however, Poulsen managed to accomplish several remarkable feats. First, he was able to tap the telephone lines of one of the foreign embassies in Los Angeles, California. It is believed this act is what led the government to believe Poulsen was dangerous. Prior to this point, there had been numerous reports filed on Poulsen, but an investigation had been put off indefinitely (Littman, 1997). Poulsen accomplished his second incredible feat when he rerouted the phone systems of a local pimp's competitors. When someone would call one of the rival pimps, the phone would ring at a location selected by Poulsen. Poulsen claimed that he originally performed this act as part of a joke to prove that he was capable of accomplishing such a feat. Within a short period of time, however, the pimp was able to increase his profits to such a level that he wanted to keep Poulsen, and his phone rerouting abilities, on permanent payroll (Littman, 1997).

Each of the aforementioned escapades led to notoriety for Poulsen, but perhaps the most notable of Poulsen's phone exploits was when he and a friend rigged a phone-in contest offered by a local radio station. By tapping into the phone lines for the radio station from a nearby apartment, the two were able to monitor the number of calls being placed to the radio station. When the appropriate number of calls had been made, Poulsen would reroute the phone lines, dial into the radio station himself, and win the grand prize - a Porsche. In the course of a one-week contest Poulsen and his accomplice were able to achieve this feat twice (Littman, 1997).

Like many in the hacker and phreaker community, Poulsen did attempt to clean up his life by getting a legitimate job in the computer science field. Ultimately, however, he was unable to keep from returning to the illegal side of computing and phone phreaking (Littman, 1997). It was perhaps Poulsen's constant return to the dark side of computing that has led many to consider him one of the most influential individuals in both the realm of hacking and phreaking. It should be noted that since his last arrest Poulsen has been leading an apparently lawful life. Currently, he serves as the editor of SecurityFocus.com, an online information security website. The escapades of Kevin Poulsen show that while phreaking is not a physically threatening crime, it can be very costly to the telecommunications industry. This in turn affects citizens since the telephone companies are forced to continue raising their rates to compensate for the financial losses caused by phone phreakers. An individual's privacy can also be affected when a phreaker hijacks a telephone system, as proven by the fact that Poulsen reportedly knew everything there was to know about his friends and neighbors.

Examining Cyber Crimes

Cyber crimes have been defined as a crime involving the use of a computer and a network in the commission of a crime (Casey, 2000). Just as in the case of computer crimes, cyber crimes are separated in this work as a means of simplifying their discussion. Crimes like that of narcotics trafficking could be considered a cyber crime because the act may be committed without the use of a computer, but a cyber crime is committed when the activities involve computers. Another mounting crime is cyber stalking. Cyber stalking refers to harassment of individuals via the Internet or e-mail that results in the victim suffering substantial emotional distress (McGraw, 1995). The latest argument concerning cyber stalking is that the crime results in censorship of women when they are forced to change the way they handle themselves when they are online (Brail, 1996). Despite the rise in frequency for these crimes, the crimes of virtual child pornography and identity theft are still considered to be two of the more commonly encountered crimes, and as such warrant consideration in this work.

Digital Child Pornography

It is commonly held that children possessed fewer legal rights in the 1800's than they do today. According to Flowers (1994), minors were considered the property of their parents and largely excluded from the safeguards of American Constitutional law. Many times children were used as workers by their parents in an attempt to supplement family income. Examples of such work include laboring in factories or fields, but occasionally the child was also subject to prostitution; this was especially the case for younger girls. Some researchers who have studied this phenomenon attribute this belief to the fact that men have always had sexual fantasies relating to young virgins (Flowers, 1994). Because few women who worked as prostitutes were of virginal character, parents were able to get good money for the prostitution of their children, both male and female in many cases.

Over the years, the desire of adults to have sexual relations with children has come to be known as pedophilia. Pedophilia has been defined as the adult fetish to make children a sexual object, normally consisting of non-violent sexual contact with a child including genital viewing or fondling, oral genital contact, penetration, or other sexual contact. Pedophilia has come to be considered one of the most common victimizations of children (Flowers, 1994).

With an increasing desire to engage children in sexual situations, individuals began the process of manufacturing and distributing child pornography. The term child pornography is used to refer to videos, books, magazines, or photos depicting children in various sexual activities. The first recorded instance of child pornography is believed to have been produced in China in the late 1400's when a sex manual entitled *The Admirable Discourses of the Plain Girl* was released (Flowers, 1994). Since this time, the field of child pornography has seen dramatic changes. Despite changes in the belief that children are property and have no rights, there has been a steady increase in the manufacture and distribution of child pornography throughout the twentieth century. According to an article on the Safe4Kids website (2002), Europeans began to mass-produce child pornography during the 1960's and 1970's. The material, which was circulated mostly from Denmark and Holland, was so widely distributed that much of the child pornography manufactured during this time is still in circulation today. In recent years Japan has emerged as a leader in the production and dissemination of child pornography (Buford, 2002).

The advent of technology has not only increased the speed and quality of child pornography production, but has also led to new forms of child pornography. Along with traditional types of child pornography, there are now electronic mass-produced types. Traditional movies and pictures have been replaced with the use of .mpeg and .avi movie formats, as well as .jpeg picture formats that depict children engaged in sexual acts. Web pages use the .mpeg format because the compression creates smaller file sizes and is better suited for the possibility of being downloaded via slower Internet connections. The .avi format is used when an individual desires a lower compression and wishes to produce a higher quality video, normally to be stored on a CD-ROM that can hold large amounts of data. The .jpeg files are highly compressed picture formats commonly used for picture files that are going to be transmitted via the Internet.

It is worth noting that these are not the only media formats that could contain child pornography. Movies files created for play on the Quicktime software player is labeled as .mov and there is also a .asf for video files. Picture files may come in .bmp, which is the windows bitmap format or .gif, which is an animated image file. The formats previously discussed are merely the more commonly encountered file formats.

The use of these electronic formats are superior to their physical counterparts in that copies can be mass produced at a speed ten times faster than physical copies, and the images never lose quality, regardless of how many times the image or video is copied. Combine this with the ease in which individuals can transfer digital images and it is entirely possible that both users and traders of child pornography will soon prefer the use of electronic formats.

Using Child Pornography in the Grooming Process

Louis Freeh (2002) has indicated that many pedophiles share and swap their collections of child pornography with others with the intent of improving their collections. Additionally, the materials may be used when a pedophile encounters a child they believe to be susceptible to the possibility of a sexual relationship. This process of establishing trust for a future relationship is referred to as the grooming process. Grooming has been defined as the process of gaining a child's trust, breaking down his or her defenses and manipulating the child into performing a desired sexual act (Weber, 2002; Wolf, 2001).

The grooming process will normally begin with an attempt by the pedophile to foster a pseudo-friendship with the child. The child victims of pedophiles are selected from a variety of areas, but schools, shopping malls and playgrounds are popular because of the large number of potential victims. Victims will also normally come from homes in which the child believes that he or she is not loved. Pedophiles often attempt to convince the child that he or she respects, understands and even loves the child. Once the child becomes comfortable with this level of contact, then the perpetrator will move to the next level of seduction, with each subsequent level becoming more and more dangerous for the child (Weber, 2002).

With a growing sense of trust developing between the child and the pedophile, the child may become convinced that the relationship is secret. This belief that the relationship is secret will many times stem from the pedophile's ability to convince the child that their parents would be upset if they knew the child was having fun with the adult. Another variation of this may involve the pedophile providing gifts to the child, and then attempting to convince the child that the parents would be upset if they discovered the child was receiving gifts. It is at this level that the pedophile may occasionally go so far as to convince the child that talking could result in someone being hurt, whether it is the child or the child's parents (Wolf, 2001).

At this point, pedophiles will examine their relationship with the child and attempt to determine whether there is an emotional bond established between them. If so, physical contact begins. The first few physical contacts will normally consist of very light touching or rubbing. Many children do not realize that their adult friend is touching him or her in a negative manner (Wolf, 2001). Weber (2002) indicates that the adult may even attempt to represent these first few touches as accidental contact. Regardless, once the physical contact begins, it is normally only a matter or time until the child becomes engaged in the commission of a sexual act.

Pedophiles may begin using their collections of child pornography around the time physical interaction begins with the child. The pornography is used to convince the child that sexual contact is normal. These pictures normally follow a pre-set pattern. The first pictures consist of images showing children merely standing around naked. These images may consist of one or more children, but each child in the image is naked and separate from the other. The next level of pictures consists of images of naked children touching each other. These pictures are of course used to convince the child there is nothing wrong with naked children touching each other. Once the pedophile believes the child has become accepting of the pictures of children touching each other, the child will be sent the final series of pictures. These final pictures will consist of children having sexual intercourse with an adult. This is the stage where the pedophile will begin attempting some form of sexual relationship with the child (Wolf, 2001).

Traditionally, the grooming process has been used in the sexual entrapment of children, but a new technique is becoming increasingly popular. Law enforcement personnel have recently seen an increase in pedophiles circumventing the children. Some pedophiles have decided that the process of gaining a child's trust can be sped up if he or she first grooms the child's parents (Burstow, 2002). Under this form of grooming, pedophiles attempt to convince parents that he or she has a genuine interest in the well being of the child. Once the parents are accepting of the relationship between the perpetrator and the child, then the pedophile will begin to groom the child. This speeds up the grooming process because the secrecy phase is eliminated. Pedophiles normally tell children that his or her parents are aware of their physical contact, or try to convince children that their parents would not believe them if they tattled. (Burstow, 2002).

Few parents understand the grooming process and therefore do not discuss the potential dangers with their children. For this reason, some have recommended that the solution to the problem may lie in involving both parents and law enforcement in a process of education that will provide children with the necessary skills to detect situations where they are being groomed and alert adults (Burstow, 2002). Developing this level of understanding is even more important when one considers that some emotional effects of the grooming process may be as damaging to a child victim as the actual sexual victimization (Still, 2003).

Child Pornography and the Internet

The advent of the Internet has only increased the problem of child pornography. According to Robert Flores, the former head of the Justice Department's anti-child-porn section, almost all of the government's remedial campaigns in the 1980's were undone within two years of the Internet's public release. During the 1980's, the government managed to cut the flow of child pornography down to where it was almost non-existent. The ease of transportation that the Internet brought forth, however, led to an increase in child pornography that makes the problem worse than it ever was in previous years. Indeed, Flores believes that the Internet has reduced the campaign against child pornography to an almost half-hearted effort (Kaplan, 1997).

Part of the problem lies in the fact that the pornography industry has been well established for centuries, with many believing the Internet is merely another method of obtaining these materials. According to one study by Dr.

Kimberly McCabe (2000) of the University of North Carolina, one-third of respondents to a survey indicated that downloading child pornography was acceptable behavior. This finding came despite the fact that over 90% of the respondents indicated they knew child pornography was illegal. McCabe contends that the reason for this discrepancy lies in the fact that some adults view juvenile sexuality as a necessary part of the maturation process. Further, the respondents that indicated support for child pornography were predominantly white males who maintained gainful employments. McCabe theorizes a correlation between acceptance of child pornography and the general acceptance of pornography by adult males (McCabe, 2000).

The advent of the Internet has created several additional problems that were not considered as recently as a decade ago. Thanks to the Internet, individuals not generally known for having enough freedom to obtain such illicit materials are reaching the child pornography industry. According to Bernstein (1997), the problem of the Internet and child pornography has become so bad that inmates in state and federal penitentiaries are now capable of collecting and distributing child pornography via the library computers. Many correctional officers and other prison personnel may not be familiar enough with the operation of computers to understand what inmates are doing while they are using a computer, and this could render correctional institutions major distribution centers for child pornography. Other government institutions and public facilities that provide clients with computers are also at risk. Internet cafes, for example, maintain computers connected to the Internet and could be used in the commission of illegal acts.

Beginning in the 1980's, bulletin board services, also known as BBSes, were increasingly used to distribute child pornography. A bulletin board service works as follows: a subscriber dials into the bulletin board service and once the computers are connected then the files can be transferred from his or her computer to the BBS operator's computer. Likewise, as files can be transferred up to the operator's computer, files can also be transferred down to the subscriber's computer. These services are normally subscription and open only to those the administrator approves.

The story of Helena became one of the most, if not the most, popular child pornography series in the world thanks to the distribution capabilities provided by these bulletin board services (Jenkins, 2001). Helena was a little girl who appeared to be 8 to 10 years old. A series of photographs depicting Helena having sex with a boy her age and an older man, who was assumed to be her father, became the most traded pictures on BBSes. Helena became known as "Hel-Lo", a call-name by which individuals could locate online photographs. Hel-Lo stood for Helena-Lolita (Jenkins, 2001), Lolita being the call-name most often associated with pornography featuring little girls. It is believed that the name comes from the classic novel *Lolita*, which was the story of a prepubescent girl who became the love interest of an older man.

Today, bulletin board services are not used as often as they were in the earlier days of the Internet. Instead, the common contemporary method of transmitting information over the Internet involves the use of a web page, and a number of Internet researchers assert that as much as 69% of all profits for web sites are generated through the sale of pornography (Casanova, 2000). Of the 40 million sites available on the Internet, there are over 1 million pornographic pictures of children available at any one time during the day (Safe4Kids, 2002). One recent development related to the issue of child pornography and the Internet is the prosecution of individuals for the possession of child pornography in a computer's cache folder (Howard, 2004). The cache folder of a hard drive is used to load images viewed by a computer's user. In the past this process was used to speed up the loading of webpages when a slow Internet connection was used. With the advent of high speed Internet connections, there is debate as to whether the cache folder is even needed today. Regardless, operating systems still provide the folder and images that are viewed during a user's online activity is stored in the folder.

In the case of *United States v. Tucker* (2001) the court was asked to determine whether child pornography images contained in the cache folder qualified as possession of child pornography. The defendant claimed that he could not possess the images because they were not downloaded to the computer. The court, however, disagreed and compared the deletion of materials, and their subsequent storage in a cache folder with the destruction of narcotics by a drug dealer. The future of this approach has been questioned by some legal scholars. As noted by Howard (2004), individuals who only view images of child pornography are not as culpable as those that download, trade, or use child pornography materials. However, at the current time it appears that mere viewing of child pornography via the Internet may still result in one's prosecution for possession of child pornography. As with many issues associated with high technology crime, the decision to proceed with such an investigation should be made on a case-by-case basis.

The increasing use of the Internet has also led to an increase in the use of electronic mail, also known as e-mail. E-mail is now the chosen method of communication for almost all Internet users in their day-to-day communications. Children are no exception. In fact, it is entirely possible that children use e-mail and the Internet more than adults, for many individuals appear to have little or no desire to learn about computers. Pedophiles, on the other hand, are fully aware of the popularity of electronic mail among minors and they will use the technology to their own ends.

The grooming process does not change significantly when a pedophile uses the Internet and e-mail during the process. Major changes come only in the methods of contact. Rather than physically visiting schoolyards, playgrounds and other child-related hang outs, pedophiles now stalk chat rooms designed for children (Book, 2004). Although not every child is susceptible to the grooming process, the fact that many children encounter pedophiles while online is a frightening consideration. Most pedophiles will enter child-topic chat rooms and strike up discussions with the children, with the adult normally being well versed in the latest in children's television and movies (Kidsap, 2002).

While most of the individuals involved in these activities are adults, researchers are finding that an increasing number of those trying to prey on minors in chat rooms are children the same age as the victims (Kidsap, 2002). Regardless of the age of the sexual predator, however, the victim is normally desensitized via e-mailed child pornography. The process of grooming via e-mail works in much the same way as grooming works in the physical world. The first pictures are of naked children, and others that progressively reveal more sexual contact between the children follow these. Once the child is fully desensitized, the perpetrator arranges a meeting with the victim. When this occurs, it is common for a "traveler case" to develop; that is, the pedophile travels across state lines to the area in which the victim lives. It is believed that a troubling number of these cases develop each and every day.

Just as the introduction of the Internet undid the work of federal law enforcement in the 1980s, the introduction of peer-to-peer networking has affected their work in the 1990s. Peer-to-peer networking is commonly referred to as P2P networking and involves the linking of two computers in order to share files, whether the files are music, video, or picture. Perhaps the best example of peer-to-peer networking software is that of the Napster music-trading software. Napster was the original file sharing or file-swapping program. A college student who desired to trade music files stored on his computer developed the program. The young man's program took advantage of the .mp3 compression, which allowed for audio files to be compressed into smaller file sizes. This was important in that prior to the use of .mp3 compression an audio file could be as large as 45 MB in size and would take anywhere from 4 to 5 hours to transfer via a modem. The same file compressed in .mp3 is around 3 MB and can be transferred in as little as ten minutes or less.

Because of repeated legal battles, the Napster Empire has fallen in recent years, but the software manufacturers that have emerged in its shadow are just as powerful, perhaps even more powerful. Peer-to-peer network software designers are no longer content to allow only the transfer of music files. New releases of peer-to-peer software allow for the transfer of any type of file on the user's computer, including the transfer of pictures, video, and software.

Peer-to-peer networking software has provided new challenges to law enforcement officers who are investigating the distribution of child pornography. Because there is no central server to which users might connect, it is almost impossible to track all users, especially since there is now one piece of software serving 2,000,000 registered users at any given time during the day. Some of the more common peer-to-peer file-sharing programs are Music City Morpheus, Bearshare, WinMx, and Limewire. Each piece of software works the same, with only minor differences in how files are transferred. For example, Music City Morpheus allows users to download any file format, and even allows users to download from multiple users. By downloading from multiple users, the transfer of a file is sped up as the program pulls bits of the data from several different users who have higher transfer speeds. Once the file is completed, then the file is assembled and ready to be opened. This is especially helpful for distributors of child pornography because they can download videos up to 6 times faster than many other peer-to-peer software users.

The fact that transfers of video files may take considerably longer to transfer does not appear to have affected the transfer of child pornography via these peer-to-peer networks. According to recent research conducted by both a representative of the U.S. House of Representatives (2001) and Sanders (2001), these peer-to-peer networks are used by a large number of children and are resulting in children swapping images of child pornography. In fact, three of the top ten most requested search terms on one of the peer-to-peer networks relates to child pornography terms. This is evidence that the trading of videos depicting child pornography may be becoming more rampant than the trading of child porn pictures.

Identity Theft

Elliot (2002) has defined identity theft as the illegal appropriation of information pertaining to an individual's personal identity – a name, a social security number or birth information. Information provided by the National White Collar Crime Center (2002) indicates that identity theft is currently the leading white-collar crime in the nation. Once an individual's information is stolen, it can be used in a number of different ways. Generally, there are three types of identity theft: physical identity theft, credit identity theft and virtual identity theft. The first type of identity theft includes the stealing of one's actual identity. This form of identity theft, while rare, has occurred in at least one high profile case. According to articles in the *Australian* (2000) and the *Los Angeles Times* (2000), a gentleman by the name of Anthony Taylor used the technique to assume the identity of Tiger Woods. Somehow, Taylor managed to obtain Tiger Woods' social security number and was able to apply for credit cards and a driver's license. For several days, Taylor lived life as Tiger Woods, actually holding himself out to be Eldrick Woods at several locations.

The second type of identity theft is the theft of someone's credit identity, which occurs when someone is able to obtain another individual's social security number and begin applying for credit under that individual's name (Newman, 1999). Unlike physical identity theft where the focus is on living the life of the victim, this second form of identity theft focuses only on establishing credit in a victim's name. This form of identity theft normally begins after personal identification information is stolen from a victim.

Such theft of information is not difficult for someone who is skilled in the craft. Sometimes skill in the theft of personal information is not even required. For example, a recent mistake in an IRS field office resulted in people receiving the wrong tax information (Lohse, 2001). This led to hundreds of individuals receiving other peoples' tax information - information that could then be used in identity theft. The Avenger (1991) lists several physical methods of obtaining information used in identity theft; these include shoulder-surfing, which is reading someone's personal information off their driver's license, checks or credit cards as they pay for their purchases at a retail establishment, and dumpster diving, which refers to the act of rummaging through the trash for credit card carbons and receipts. Some in the business world argue that the dumpster diving technique is no longer applicable because few businesses still use the credit card carbons. The truth, however, is that many still use devices that print an individual's entire credit card number and name on it, and with this information an identity thief is still just as well off as if they had found a credit card carbon. With just a few numbers from an actual credit card, it is possible for an individual to obtain a software program that will generate a credit card number for short-term use (Zaenglein, 2000).

Virtual identity theft occurs when someone steals another individual's online identity. Understanding of this new form of identity theft requires a brief discussion on the composition of an online identity. When an individual establishes an e-mail account, he or she is required to provide a user name. Normally, the user name is not the individual's actual name but instead is a virtual identity; this is the result of so many people being online today. Virtual identity theft occurs when someone cracks the password of a user and then begins to send out e-mails that are harassing or sexually suggestive under this individual's name. This leads all original investigations back to the unknowing user.

A recent article by Sigal (2002) touched upon this issue when he related a case of identity theft and a resulting lawsuit filed by a user against the Internet service provider America Online, which has long been listed on numerous hacker websites as having one of the easiest password encryptions to crack. The family involved in the case was suing America Online because the daughter's account password had been cracked and the perpetrator was sending out sexually suggestive e-mails claiming to be the little girl. The perpetrator, who has not yet been located, also created an online profile for the little girl and listed one of her favorite hobbies as sex. An on-line profile is in essence a data sheet stored in America Online's computers. Other users can search the profiles database for individuals who are from the same geographic area, others who share interests and others who share hobbies. Many adults and children hang out in America Online chat rooms discussing sex and what the individuals would like to do to each other. This profile resulted in numerous harassing instant messages and e-mails. The father filed the lawsuit claiming that America Online failed to reasonably protect his daughter's good name.

The Growing Problem of Identity Theft

The crime of identity theft is rarely a physically dangerous crime. Identity theft normally results in financial loss or damage to a victim's reputation. Reputation may be damaged if identity is stolen and the thief uses it to commit minor legal infractions. This form of identity theft has been documented in several cases. In the case of Christian Richards, a young man was sent over 20 speeding and moving violation tickets and summonses for failure to appear in court (Wright, 2001). When Richards informed the court that he had never owned a driver's license, it was determined that someone had stolen his identity and registered a car in his name. Each time the individual was stopped while driving the illegally registered automobile, he would claim he did not have his license with him and the officer would ticket him based on the vehicle's registration.

Many times the perpetrators of identity theft operate out of very inconspicuous locations. For example, it was recently reported that convicts under the jurisdiction of the Florida Department of Corrections operated an identity theft ring from inside the confines of a prison. Using a combination of outside prison contacts and telephone communications from within, the prison ring was able to commit around $200,000 worth of fraud and identity theft. It is believed that the ring could have continued indefinitely if one of the victims had not complained after they were served with a summons for failure to appear in court in a case involving failure to return a rental vehicle (Hallifax, 2001).

Another high profile case of identity theft was that of Donald McNeese. McNeese, a former employee of Prudential Insurance Company, stole a personnel listing with over 60,000 individuals' names, social security information and other personal information such as addresses. The list was then sold via numerous online chat rooms and Internet relay chat sessions. It is unknown how many of the personnel listings were sold before law enforcement agencies were able to put a stop to McNeese's activities (Hopper, 2002).

Identity theft is not only considered one of the more damaging crimes, but also the fastest growing of the high technology crimes. Information released by the Federal

Trade Commission indicates that identity theft accounts for more than 40 percent of all consumer fraud complaints, with somewhere between 500,000 and 700,000 reports of identity theft collected by various law enforcement agencies and consumer groups in 2001 (National White Collar Crime Center, 2002). According to David Doege (2002), a researcher for a Milwaukee news journal, identity theft is rampant because victims can come from any social or racial class. Whether the victim is young or old, rich or poor, if the identity thief can obtain the necessary personal information, an individual becomes susceptible. In fact, Doege contends that identity theft is the easiest of the high technology crimes.

The ease in which identity theft can be committed could be responsible for the fact that identity theft has already established itself as one of the most financially devastating of technology crimes. Last year identity theft claims led to over $1 billion in lost funds for public and private corporations. These numbers are even more frightening when one considers that many individuals do not discover they have been victimized until months after the crime has been committed. Additionally, many who finally do discover they have been victimized may never report their identity theft cases (Hopper, 2002). There have been no specific reasons provided for why individuals do not report the crimes. It is possible that victims do not believe that law enforcement is willing or able to handle the investigation. Another possible reason for lack of reporting is that individuals may not realize under federal law they are only responsible for a portion of the illegal transactions if they report the abuse.

One common misunderstanding is that identity theft is the result of giving out information over the Internet to online retailers. While it is a good idea to be cautious when giving out personal information over the Internet, the truth is that only a small percentage of identity theft victims are victimized because of inputting information into online retail websites (Verton, 2001). The reality is that the technical ability and time required for these activities are so great that the majority of identity thieves would rather just hack into a computer and steal listings of credit cards, a problem that has increased dramatically in recent years.

Insurance companies have also begun to accept that the problem of identity theft is not going to disappear. Beginning in early April 2002, a Virginia insurance company began selling identity theft insurance for $25,000. The company does not argue that credit card companies will not work with their cardholders in situations where there is an identity theft encountered. Instead, it is the insurance company's contention that the hardest part, and the most expensive, is the completion of papers necessary to get someone's credit identity restored. This policy provides funds intended to relieve the financial burdens associated with repairing one's credit (Bonisteel, 2002).

Until recently, most law enforcement agencies did not deal directly with the investigation of identity theft complaints. Instead, when an individual claimed to be a victim of identity theft, law enforcement agencies would merely mail out a victim's packet. This packet was nothing more than a self-report statement indicating what exactly happened and how much money was lost as a result of the identity theft. The packet would generally be received within a week, but by this point most identity thieves had moved to newer victims. Not only was the slow response time a problem for investigation of the crime, victims in many areas could also not begin repairing their credit until they received an official copy of a complaint filed with a law enforcement agency (Campbell, 2002).

Many states have now modified their laws to require law enforcement officers to make timely reports in cases of identity theft. These laws have been developed in an attempt to aid citizens who are victims of identity theft and need an official police report in order to begin repairing their credit. Since the passage of the new law, police departments have reported an incredible increase in the number of claims that they receive every week (Tran, 2001).

Identity theft is one of the harder high technology crimes for law enforcement to investigate because it is just beginning to occur at equal rates in both the physical and online worlds. Physical identity theft, while difficult to investigate, can be investigated using traditional police investigative techniques. Online identity thefts present a far greater problem because law enforcement officers are normally not trained to follow the cyber-trail, which has been defined as the trail of evidence that exists in cyberspace or contained on various storage mediums that are digital in nature (Casey, 2000).

There is a growing trend toward the development of better-trained computer forensics experts who can handle such complex investigations, but due to financial limitations, there are few of these individuals outside of major metropolitan police departments. Hence, many credit card companies are attempting to reduce the number of identity theft claims by implementing new technology. Visa recently unveiled its Verified by Visa program where online consumers select a password and are required to enter it in order to use the credit card at participating web sties (Goldstein, 2002).

The government has introduced new legislation that could assist in the prevention of identity theft. Recently Senator Dianne Feinstein began seeking support for new legislation that would limit the amount of personal information printed on credit card receipts and penalizes credit agencies that do not take adequate precautions to protect individuals from identity theft (Hopper, 2002). Further, the state of California has recently restricted the sale of birth and death records because the sales were not being verified to ensure that identity thieves were not purchasing the records (Stamberg, 2001).

Some of the better-financed law enforcement departments have begun hiring officers who are trained in computer forensics to assist in identity theft investigations. A recent article in the *Australian* (2002) discussed the duties of these employees. Abraham Abdallah, age 32, used his cellular phone and computer to collect personal information about over half of Forbes' top 400 richest men. Yet, it took the New York City police department's cyber crime expert over two years to track him down. Along with credit card information, Abdallah managed to gather bank codes and brokerage accounts for individuals such as Oprah Winfrey and George Soros. Abdallah, a high school dropout, was employed as a kitchen hand at a small restaurant while he was committing these crimes.

Past Responses to High Technology Crime

Law enforcement has traditionally been slow to respond to advances in technology, and this has led to the formation of several vigilante hacker groups that have targeted technology crimes like child pornography. In fact, a contest at one time developed among several hacker groups, with each trying to outdo the other in shutting down websites related to inappropriate activity such as child pornography (Radcliff, 2000). Once the groups were made aware of a possible problem with child pornography, they notified the FBI and local law enforcement, as well as the offender's Internet Service Provider. If action was not forthcoming then the groups would take matters into their own hands, gaining access to the suspect's computer and then erasing all of the illegal materials from the hard drive of the computer (Radcliff, 2000). Many Internet Service Providers have claimed that any individual caught transmitting illegal materials or using their services to engage in other illegal behavior will be banned. However, there are some who doubt the truthfulness of such claims (Platt, 1997).

The fact that these cyber vigilantes are in operation has been met with varying responses from individuals in the law enforcement community. Many law enforcement officers believe that child pornography is such a horrible crime that they have no problem with hackers violating the sanctity of the suspect's computer. Others believe that to allow the cyber vigilantes to continue would merely encourage the existence of physical vigilantes, which almost all would agree to be an unacceptable action (Radcliff, 2000).

Radcliff (2000) makes mention of yet another problem law enforcement agencies face when a vigilante hacker group attacks a suspect's computer – loss of potential evidence. When hacker groups attack a web site, the normal procedure is for the hackers to delete the contents of the suspect's hard drive. Deleting information does not mean that the information is gone forever and cannot be retrieved; however, it does make it considerably harder for law enforcement to garner evidence against the alleged perpetrators.

Because few law enforcement agencies are able to hire computer technicians to handle the investigations of high technology crimes, several software companies have begun offering new tools that aid in the investigation of electronically distributed child pornography. VisualRoute is one such new tool and works off the same concept as Traceroute, with Traceroute allowing one individual to track another individual's IP address. An IP address is an identifying number assigned to a particular user each time he or she connects to the Internet. There are two types of IP addresses: static and dynamic. Dynamic is the harder of the two for law enforcement to investigate since every time an individual connects to the Internet via their service provide they receive a different IP address. Static is more common in broadband connections affiliated with companies or universities and are easier to investigate because an individual maintains the same IP address every time he or she connects to the Internet. Traceroute tracks the location of a particular IP address, while VisualRoute simplifies this process even further by displaying an actual map and pinpointing on the map the exact location of the suspect's computer (Moad, 2001).

Another technique discussed by Kaplan (1997) is the establishment of a "honey pot" to attract potential child pornography addicts. A honey pot is commonly used in the field of computer security to describe a website that is established solely as a means of being attractive and identifying perpetrators. Law enforcement officers working for the U.S. Customs Service recently applied this technique, establishing a fake child pornography website (Kaplan, 1997). The website attracted more than 70,000 hits in the course of the first two months. By offering users access to child pornography, and then requiring them to sign up to swap child pornography with others visiting the website, law enforcement was able to locate thousands of child pornographers by either their subscription information or their IP address. The main draw in this operation was of course access to the largest porn collection in the world, the

United States Customs Office's collection. Because of their numerous years of investigations, Customs has amassed the largest collection of child pornography anywhere, and child porn collectors were so eager to gain access to such a large volume of material that they did not realize they could be deceived until it was too late (Kaplan, 1997).

Another technique used by law enforcement to track down child pornographers is the use of electronic surveillance. The FBI's Operation Innocent Images frequently uses this technique. Using a court order, agents of the FBI can intercept electronic communications. This technique was originally intended to allow law enforcement to track not only the collectors of child pornography but the distributors as well. The use of electronic interception techniques has not been without problems. It has been estimated that 840 subscribers of AOL have been accidentally ensnared in the FBI's electronic surveillance in recent years (Fuentes, 1996).

The tools are getting easier for law enforcement officials to operate, but there remain several problems. According to Ko (2002), a recent investigation conducted by a private investigator in Canada uncovered proof that several supposed child pornography "investigators" were actually pedophiles who were using their job as a means of viewing child pornography at their discretion. To combat this problem, legislation has been introduced in Canada that would prohibit investigators from viewing child pornography even when they are on the job. There appears to be no documentation that supports the belief that this is a widespread problem, but it does not appear to be merely a Canadian phenomenon. U.S. Customs and the FBI's Operation Innocent Images indicate that several pedophiles under watch are either active military or law enforcement (Ko, 2002). Another recent development that has affected the investigation of virtual child pornography is the recent Supreme Court decision of *Ashcroft v. Free Speech Coalition* (2002). Under the ruling, law enforcement officers who investigate the crime of child pornography are responsible for providing proof that the images seized are those of actual child pornography. Law enforcement agencies that now investigate crimes involving child pornography are required to prove that videos do not contain adults who are attempting to portray children engaged in sexual acts. When dealing with pictures involving child pornography, investigators are required to prove that the child in the picture is actually a child. Due to advancements in digital technology, it is now possible to generate a fake picture that appears to be a child but is in fact a computer-generated image. This places a rather stringent requirement on investigators, as they must now discover ways to verify that the image is that of an actual child engaged in sexual activity.

There are two potential methods of verifying that images contain actual children engaged in illegal activities. The first method is by examination of the image using enhancement software. This technique involves using digital equipment to ensure that the image originally included in the picture has not been modified nor had additional images added. By enlarging the image and looking for blurring or smudging indicative of doctoring, investigators can ensure that the child depicted in an image is in fact a child (Wayner, 2002). The problem with this technique is that as technology gets better, it is possible that a superior enhancement program could be developed. If this were to happen, then this technique could be removed from use.

A second method of verifying that a potential image contains actual child pornography involves comparing the image to a database of images collected by the United States Customs Service. This method is workable but problematic for two reasons. First, while the Customs database is exhaustive, individuals who use child pornography may engage in the manufacture of their own images, thereby rendering the Customs database useless. Second, if every state and local law enforcement agency begins to ask the U.S. Customs Service for assistance, it is only a matter of time before the agency will have to deny help because of a lack of resources.

One technological advancement that is helping with this endeavor is the development of computer forensics software that allows users to compare images they obtain from a digital storage medium with images from the Customs database, or with other state law enforcement agencies' databases. Using mathematical applications, the characters in these files are assigned a hash value. The evidence media is then hashed and the hash library from known child pornography images is compared to the evidence media (Guidance Software, 2002). Currently, there are few who have used this technique, but it certainly may have an impact upon future child pornography investigations.

According to the operators of Operation Blue Ridge Thunder (2002), the most effective means of preventing child pornography lies in education – a process they call target hardening. This merely means that potential victims of high technology crimes should be provided with proper education to ensure that if they are still victims, they are not easy victims. Educating potential victims may take one of several formats, but the best education comes in the format of training seminars and publications for parents and potential victims. Numerous anti-child pornography agencies provide publications and seminars addressing the dangers of child pornography and unsolicited contact online. Agencies like the National White Collar Crime Center have released guidelines on how to be aware of, and to prevent, identity theft. Law enforcement agencies should consider working with these agencies to harden potential targets in their jurisdiction.

Some researchers have recommended the use of Internet monitoring programs to protect children from predators online. These programs work by denying children access to certain websites that are stored in the program's listings, or the program may prevent the child from transferring files from computer to computer (Akdeniz, 1999).

If workable, these programs would be an excellent method of protecting children; however, many of them do not work for two reasons. First, the listing that these programs operate cannot keep up with the number of Internet sites that spring up between the purchase of the software and the use of the software, and most of the programs do attempt to provide updates. Second, the children who are using the software may be more computer literate than their parents and can reprogram the protections to allow for unlimited Internet access.

Emerging Law

Enacted by Congress in the wake of the terrorist attacks of September 11, 2001, on New York and Washington, D.C., the USA PATRIOT Act is one of the most recent laws impacting cyber crime. The statute was enacted for the express purpose of strengthening the investigation powers and prosecutorial powers involved in the investigation of terrorist acts. The act, however, has not been met without criticism, as the Electronic Freedom Foundation and the organization Truthout have published a series of sharp criticisms on the act.

Section 220, which deals with the nationwide service of search warrants for electronic evidence, allows for a search warrant concerning the seizure of electronic communications issued in one district to be enforceable nationwide. America Online (AOL) is perhaps the largest Internet service provider and is located out of the state of Virginia. Prior to the passage of the USA PATRIOT Act, law enforcement officers were required to obtain search warrants from a magistrate from the state and district in which AOL operates. Today, however, a judge in any state can issue a search warrant that is recognizable in the state of Virginia. The Electronic Freedom Foundation (EFF) maintains that this warrant need not identify the particular service provider in the warrant, but if this provision exists then it is a little known section and was not found by this author (EFF, 2002).

Section 216, which deals with the modification of authorities relating to use of pen registers and trap and traced devices, provides assistance for law enforcement officers who wish to execute roving wiretaps on potential suspects. This is accomplished by adding the phrase "or trap and trace device" after "pen register" in Section 3121(c) of title 18, U.S.C. , inserting ", routing, addressing" after "dialing" and striking "call processing" and inserting "the processing and transmitting of wire or electronic communications so as not to include the contents of any wire or electronic communications". Hence, law enforcement may legally monitor both voice and electronic communication, including communication via the Internet.

Furthermore, under Section 216 (b) (a) (1) of the Act, a court order can authorize the installation and use of a pen register or trap and trace device anywhere in the United States, once the court finds that the government's attorney has provided sufficient proof that the evidence that could be obtained is relevant to an ongoing criminal investigation. Moreover, the government is merely required to show that the information *could* be relevant. So a pen register or trap and trace device can be issued on reasonable suspicion, as opposed to probable cause previously required. Further, section 216 (b) (a) (2) provides that a state investigator or state law enforcement officer can make an application for a court order authorizing the installation of a pen register or trap and trace device within any court of jurisdiction. Once again, the state investigator merely has to show that the information could potentially contribute to an ongoing investigation. Should the government, however, attempt to use its own device in place of the communication provider's, the state must provide a complete record of all transactions involved in the implementation and upkeep of the monitoring device (EFF, 2002).

Section 206 modifies the roving surveillance authority under the Foreign Intelligence Surveillance Act of 1978 to include the use of roving wiretaps when "in circumstances where the Court finds that the actions of the target of the application may have the effect of thwarting the identification of a specified person". This means that individuals under surveillance authorized by the Foreign Intelligence Act may have all of their communications, both physical and electronic, monitored.

Most of the aforementioned sections, while involving electronic communications, deal more directly with terrorist activities. Other sections of the act involve the criminalization of computer intrusions. The original format of the bill included the crime of hacking in the definition of terrorism and made it punishable by life in prison without possibility of parole. According to the Electronic Freedom Foundation (2002), this was overturned because of their numerous complaints to legislators concerning this possibility of labeling computer hacking a terrorist activity. Although the crime was not moved under the definition of terrorist activity, the Computer Fraud and Abuse Act (CFAA) of 1986 was modified by the USA PATRIOT Act's section 814, which is considered the deterrence and prevention of cyberterrorism portion of the act. Under this section, cyberterrorism is defined as conduct that causes one of the following:

(a) loss to 1 or more persons during any 1-year period (and, for purposes of an investigation, prosecution, or other proceeding brought by the United States only, loss resulting from a related course of conduct affecting 1 or more other protected computers) aggregating at least $5,000 in value.

(b) The modification or impairment, or potential modification or impairment, of the medical examination, diagnosis, treatement, or care of 1 or more individuals.

(c) Physical injury to any person.

(d) A threat to public health or safety.

(e) Damage affecting a computer system used by or for a government entity in furtherance of the administration of justice, national defense, or national security.

These provisions apply to incidents that involve acts of computer hacking and to those that attempt to engage in acts of computer intrusion. It will be interesting to see how a potential act of hacking will be tried in court, as punishment under this section requires that law enforcement prove that had the individual completed the act of hacking. Each of the requirements for cyber terrorism requires that the computer hacker either have harmed a person or caused some form of loss due to the intrusion. It is possible for an individual to illegally access a computer system without damaging the system. Does this act then allow for the prosecution of what could have been, and how can it ever truly be shown what was the individual's intent? These are all questions that law enforcement could face in the future as acts of cyber terrorism see increased use and consideration.

Several computer intrusions remained under the definition of terrorist activities, even in the final version of the USA PATRIOT Act. For example, violations of 18 USC §1030, have been labeled acts of terrorism if one of the following occurs:

(a) the individual in question accessed restricted or classified information on computers that require protection for reasons of national security, national defense or of the Atomic Energy Act of 1954 with reason to believe that the information could injure the US or advantage a foreign nation, and who willfully communicates the information to one not entitled to it, (18 USC §1030 (a) (1))

(b) violations of 18 USC §1030 that resulted in damage that causes medical care problems, physical injury, public health or safety, or

(c) affects computer system used by or for a government entity in furtherance of the administration of justice, national defense, or national security (18 USC §1030 (a)(5)(A)(i))

The aforementioned sections of the USA PATRIOT Act are not the only ones that will see increased discussion in future years, as the actual text version of the act is over 300 pages long. According to the Electronic Freedom

Foundation (2002), the powers worked into the bill have little or nothing to do with the investigation of terrorist activities. Instead, it is their contention that the law enforcement powers are ones that many in Washington have tried unsuccessfully to pass in recent years, only to find that the solution to passing the powers lied in hiding the information within emotional legislation.

A sharp criticism of the legislation relates to the events surrounding the passage of the act. During one of the congressional hearings concerning the need for new legislation a bomb threat was called in; an event that surely lead to additional emotion during the time of the hearings (Donahue & Walsh, 2001). Prior to the passage of the final legislation, which was short titled USA PATRIOT Act, there were several versions of the anti-terrorist legislation argued. There were several reasons for the success of the USA PATRIOT Act, but perhaps one of the greatest strengths in the bill was its self-imposed time limit. Prior legislation contained no time limit on the vast new powers that would be imparted upon law enforcement personnel.

The passage of the USA PATRIOT Act will present interesting debates among those in the criminal justice system in the near future, as the legislation appears to have been passed on pure emotion. Emotion may be important during the legislation process, but to pass legislation on the heels of emotion is a dangerous maneuver, and one that can only result in problems. According to Donahue and Walsh (2001), the legislation was not even read in its entirety until after the legislation was passed. The reasoning for legislators voting without reading the entire act is that not one congressman desired to let their constituents believe they were soft on terrorism. Many in the Electronic Freedom Foundation have questioned whether the USA PATRIOT Act truly accomplishes what it was designed to accomplish. For example, the act was written to handle the investigation and prosecution of terrorist activities, yet the written USA PATRIOT Act contains no clear definition of an act of terrorism. It would seem that well thought out legislation would have examined this detail a bit farther and provided a better coverage of the important issues to be handled by the act.

Only time will tell how the courts decide to interpret the legislation, but there is a rather great possibility that one of the legal arguments against the USA PATRIOT Act will involve the vagueness to which it refers to acts of terrorism. Section 216 has been sharply critiqued by the EFF because of what the organization has determined to be vague wording. It is their contention that the legislation could potentially be used to monitor the visitation of website "addresses" and other URLs that could potentially be used to identify required information (EFF, 2002). Additionally, the EFF (2002) has stated their belief that section 206 should be overturned because there is a provision allowing for the use of roving wiretaps that raises serious Fourth Amendment violations because it relaxes the "particularity" requirement of the Fourth Amendment.

Others claim that the first legal arguments will be against the amount of civil liberties violations the act allows for in cases where terrorism is believed to be involved in the criminal activity; under the passed version of the act there is little in the form of a final definition of "terrorist activity" (Donahue & Walsh, 2001). Many believe that this vagueness will present a situation in which law enforcement personnel will not be able to restrain themselves in the future. There is at least one positive aspect for individuals who would argue against the powers granted law enforcement by the USA PATRIOT Act. The act provides for several of the features to evaporate after

December 2005. Not all sections evaporate, as many of the sections dealing with the modifications of the ECPA and the amount of information that may be obtained via the various levels of process have no sunset provision (EFF, 2002).

The Volatile Nature of Digital Evidence

The very nature of evidence associated with technology-assisted crime is different. Very few technology crimes leave physical evidence at the scene of the crime. The majority of these crimes leave a trail of digital evidence, referred to by Casey (2000) as the cyber trail. Digital evidence has been defined as evidence stored on electronic media such as hard drives, floppy disks or other magnetic storage devices. The cyber trail then is the collection of electronic communications, files on a computer or any other forms of digital media (Casey, 2000).

Many people are under the assumption that when files are deleted, they are gone forever. In actuality, the files are not erased but are instead merely altered in a manner that the computer's operating system knows the space is open and can be used to save another file (Wall & Paroff, 2004). An operating system is a series of commands that control the general functions of a computer. It is the operating system that allows users to start up the computer and immediately begin running programs. In the early days of computing, a user had to load an operating system into the computer's memory via a floppy disk. Once the operating system was functional, then other programs were launched. Today, the operating system is stored on the internal hard drive of the computer. Two of the more famous operating systems are Microsoft's Windows Operating System and Red Hat's Linux Operating System.

When dealing with a deleted file, the operating system distinguishes the file from the original file through the use of the hexadecimal symbol "E5" (see figure one below). Upon making notice of the E5 designation, the file space is considered available and the system saves the new file over the old file. This, however, does not always mean that the original file is completely overwritten; many times only a portion of the file is overwritten (Casey, 2000).

Figure One: A Comparison of Original File Names and Deleted File Names

The Original File Name	The "Deleted" File Name
Resume.doc	E5csume.doc
Budget.xls	E5udget.xls

A more detailed understanding of how files are handled by a computer involves an understanding of how files are saved on a magnetic media such as hard drives or floppy disks. Storage media is comprised of several data storage tracks that run around the inside of the disk. On each one of these tracks are many smaller storage areas known as clusters. A cluster is nothing more than a grouping of storage areas on a storage media. The size of a cluster will depend upon the operating system being used. Suppose that each cluster is made up of 16 bits, with one bit being equal to one character. When a file 32 bits in size is stored on a hard drive, or any digital media, the file will take up two entire clusters. Later, if the file is erased and another file that is only 20 bits is saved over the first 32 bits, there still remains 12 bits of the original file. This area between the newly saved file's ending and the beginning file's space is known as slack space (Casey, 2000; Mandia & Prosise, 2002) (see figure two below). Because many individuals do not realize the additional 12 bits are still stored on the hard drive, the slack space is a great source for digital evidence to be recovered. Examples of information that could be discovered are passwords or personal account information (Seward & Austin, 2004).

Figure Two: An Examination of File Slack Space

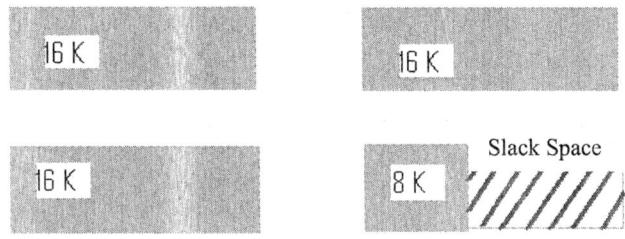

Notice the first file is 32 K in size and requires two 16 K clusters. However, after file one is erased the second file saved over it is only 24 K in size. The remaining 8 K is not erased but is instead stored inside the remaining space in the cluster. This space (8 K in the current example) is known as slack space.

Individuals who are not familiar with how computers store files and are not trained in the recovery of evidence from slack space should be careful when handling a seized computer. Failure to do so could result in damage to the evidence. It is recommended that investigators always work off of an image of a suspect's storage media. There are several disk copy programs available on the market today, with many having the capability to generate a bit-by-bit copy of the suspect media. These programs, unlike traditional copy utilities, will copy every bit of evidence and not just the active files. Traditional copy utilities will only copy the files stored on the disk and will not copy any file that is labeled with the E5 designation, resulting in the possibility of lost evidence. Traditional copy programs also fail to copy the bits that are stored in the slack space, and thus the copy, or imaged hard drive, will contain neither the previously deleted files nor any of the random data that could be recovered from the slack space. Two examples of programs capable of making a bit-by-bit copy are EnCase, which is a computer forensics program capable of full analysis of electronic media and Safeback, which is a program strictly for copying suspect media.

Thanks to advances in storage technology, hard drives are coming with larger and larger capacities. For this reason an individual can no longer expect to back up a suspect's drive using floppy disks. As recent as ten years ago, the size of hard drives was at a level that they could be copied onto floppy disks. When hard drives started to increase in size, the zip disk was invented and recommended for making images of suspect media. However, zip disks are capable of storing between 100 megabytes and 1 gigabyte of data. With the size of today's hard drives, it would take from 40 to 200 of the 1 gigabyte zip disks.

These changes have led computer forensic manufacturers to reconsider how disk imaging and copying could be completed. To solve this problem, portable computer forensic kits are now occasionally used. These units are capable of storing as much data as the largest hard drive manufactured today, and operate by connecting one hard drive, the suspect's hard drive, to another hard drive, the forensic tool kit hard drive. To make this process easier for inexperienced users, several of the computer forensic software manufactures have begun developing a kit that is capable of easily connecting the suspect hard drive to the forensic computer. One advantage of this is that the suspect computer can be left in the custody of the suspect. As will be discussed later in this work, this approach may become necessary in cases where the computer is used in the regular course of business. Other software manufacturers now allow for images of a suspect drive to be made through the use of a serial port, an outlet on a computer that is used to connect peripheral devices (Guidance Software, 2002). The benefit to using this type of connection is that the casing on the computer does not have to be removed, allowing for an easier disk imaging process and requiring even less formal knowledge of the internal workings of computers. The downside is that this form of imaging is incredibly time consuming.

Integrity of Digital Evidence

Integrity of evidence is important in every criminal case, and never is integrity more important than in the area of digital evidence. Because of the volatile nature of digital evidence, which can be changed or deleted with the push of a few keys, integrity of evidence may be harder to prove (Simon & Jones, 2004). Therefore, investigators must take every step to ensure that the original digital evidence is not altered during the examination (Brenner, 2004).

The first issue to be aware of involves the opening of a computer file. Whenever a file is opened the access times maintained by the operating system and associated with the file will change. It is for this reason that it is always recommended that an investigation involve the use of a copy of the suspect media and not the original storage media. By using a copy of the suspect media, the access times on the original will remain the same as the suspect's last accessing of the file. Advances in computer forensics technology are such that authentication of access times is almost unnecessary. However, there is little doubt that a defense attorney would make a desperate attempt to discredit evidence in such a manner.

Another method of confirming that evidence has not been changed during the course of the investigation involves the use of a hash value, which is a value assigned to a file on the basis of a mathematic algorithm. The value is computed on the basis of a bit-by-bit examination of the file. Therefore, any changes made to the file will result in a change in the hash value. According to Casey (2000) and Kruse & Heiser (2002), the creation of a hash value will normally assist investigators in proving there was no tampering with the evidence. All three researchers agree that as of today the MD5 algorithm creates the best hash value. The MD5 algorithm works as follows:

(1) First, the original file is assigned an encrypted value. Examine how the sentence below is encrypted.
The drop off site will be the corner
6b605a8x218ac7923kl73c8082c52919
(2) Once the MD5 value is assigned then any copies of the file will contain the exact MD5 value.
Copy 1: 6b605a8x218ac7923kl73c8082c52919
Copy 2: 6b605a8x218ac7923kl73c8082c52919
(3) Should any data in the file change, the MD5 value will change as well. Examine the following.
Copy 1: The drop off site will be the corner
6b605a8x218ac7923kl73c8082c52919
Copy 2: The drop off site will be McDonalds.
2l502c8d206io6391zm29a7372e87032

These procedures assure that any suspect who claims the evidence was altered by investigators can have his argument silenced by presentation of the MD5 hash value.

This method is useful because of the fact that if investigators have not altered the evidence, the original file and the copied file will contain the exact same MD5 value. While Kruse and Heiser (2002) support the use of MD5, they predict that in the near future there will be a superior, more appropriate, encryption technique.

The MD5 algorithm creates a new encrypted value for every file. Like any mathematical technique, there is always the chance of a duplicated result. However, the results of the MD5 algorithm have been shown to be more accurate than a DNA test, which is commonly accepted in court (Mercer, 2004). Therefore, if the MD5 algorithm has been properly used, then this should be sufficient proof that the files and data have not been altered in the course of the investigation.

The creation of hash values with the MD5 algorithm is normally conducted using computer forensics software. There are several accepted computer forensics applications available, but the two most accepted are probably EnCase and Safeback. EnCase is considered by many to be the most user-friendly because of the program's use of GUI (Graphical User Interface) (Guidance Software, 2002). EnCase is also one of the few computer forensics applications to have been challenged in court and found to be acceptable under the rules established in *Daubert v. Merrill Dow Pharmaceuticals* (1993), governing the admission of scientific evidence in federal trials, and *Frye v. United States* (1923), which governs the admission of scientific evidence in state trials. The manufacturers of each of the computer forensics software programs offer training for law enforcement officers and private businesses (Guidance Software, 2002). Individuals who choose to use the EnCase software may elect to achieve EnCase Certification by completing three core courses in the use of the software and undergoing an exam. This certification may be extremely helpful for law enforcement officers who wish to insure their consideration as an expert witness in cases involving computer-related crime. An in-depth understanding of computer forensics and computer forensics software is not necessary for an individual to investigate crimes involving technology, but there is at least one positive benefit to such an understanding. If investigators understand the process of forensic recovery, they will be more likely to take adequate steps to ensure that all digital evidence is properly secured at the crime scene. The manufacturers of EnCase, Guidance Software, provide an introductory course that meets this minimum level of understanding. Courses like the one offered by Guidance Software allow an investigator to better understand how digital evidence is handled by a computer or other technological device and benefits individuals who encounter this form of evidence.

CHAPTER III

Search Warrants for Digital Evidence

> *The right of the people to be secure in their persons, houses, papers, and effects, against unreasonable searches and seizures, shall not be violated, and no warrants shall issue, but upon probable cause, supported by oath or affirmation, and particularly describing the place to be searched, and the persons or things to be seized.*
>
> --- Fourth Amendment ---

When the founding fathers drafted the Fourth Amendment of the United States Constitution, they could not have foreseen all of the future technological advances that would come. Yet, this eighteenth-century declaration of the rights of persons remains immutable, and as such is the standard by which the courts evaluate the constitutionality of twenty-first century evidence.

For the Fourth Amendment to be invoked an individual must show two things. First, the individual must show that they maintain an expectation of privacy in the area that is to be searched, and second, it must be shown that that expectation of privacy is one that society is willing to accept as reasonable (McChrystal, Gleisner, & Kluborn, 1998). So, the keyword in the Fourth Amendment becomes "unreasonable," and what makes a search unreasonable is a question often debated. According to several legal scholars the easiest way to ensure that a search and seizure is not unreasonable in the eyes of the courts is to ensure that a properly drafted search warrant is used. Further, this warrant should meet the requirements of particularity and scope in regards to the items to be searched and seized (Kerr, 2001; Baron-Evans & Murphy, 2003). Numerous cases have been decided in recent years concerning the particularity and scope of a search warrant in relation to digital evidence taken from computers or other electronic devices. Regrettably, there is little in terms of final authority on the subject. Because the Supreme Court has not ruled on either of the issues, the sometimes conflicting opinions of the lower courts must be applied. Agencies that are operating within judicial circuits that have already decided several of these issues may have already been provided guidance. Agencies outside of those circuits, however, may soon encounter a case of first impression concerning technology and the Fourth Amendment.

In examining the particularity requirement of the Fourth Amendment, it generally has been held that a search warrant must contain sufficient descriptions of the places and items to be seized. This is a major consideration in cases involving computers and digital evidence. Advances in recent years have brought mediums capable of massive data storage on physically smaller disks. Today, one CD-ROM can store as much as 500 times the data of traditional floppy disks. Further, individuals using computers in the commission of criminal acts can store records on multiple disks as a means of protecting the information. Thus, a crucial question arises: when law enforcement officers request search warrants, should they include not only the computer, but all of the surrounding disks as well?

In *U.S. v. Hunter* (1998), the court held that a search warrant calling for the seizure of all computers, storage devices and software was a catchall warrant that failed to meet the particularity requirement. According to several law enforcement training materials provided as a guide for the seizure of digital evidence, the proper wording to satisfy the particularity of a search warrant includes all believed digital storage mediums as well as the phrase "including but not limited to". However, in *Matter of Search Warrant for K-Sports Imports, Inc.* (1995), the court found that the inclusion of the phrase "including but not limited to" made the warrant too vague to satisfy the particularity requirement. The issue in question in the *K-Sports* case was whether law enforcement officers could view a company's business records. Despite the government's contention that this was not their intent, the court felt that the warrant was overly broad and did not meet the requirements established by the Fourth Amendment.

Conversely, other courts have held that the particularity requirement of the Fourth Amendment is not violated when law enforcement officers make requests to search for all computer devices and computer-related storage devices. In the case of *United States v. Upham* (1999)[1], the court found

---

[1] *United States v. Upham*, 168 F.3d 532 (1st Cir. 1999) – here defendant argued that seizure of all computer equipment was overly broad and therefore invalidated the search warrant. The court disagreed finding that the warrant's indication of searching all computers was necessary to obtain the illegal images for which the warrant was issued. The court also refused to remove the images that were recovered using the "undelete" utilities. In the opinion of the court, the recovery of deleted computer evidence is equivalent to the reassembly of a ransom note and is permissible by law.

that a search for all computer related storage devices was not overly broad because the officers had to search everything to ensure they found the pertinent evidence for which they were searching. It was the belief of the court that the officers had proven they did not intend to search for personal records when they applied for the search warrant.

The scope of a search warrant is also a disputed issue. In the case of *United States v. Carey* (1999), the court found that an officer had exceeded the scope of his search warrant for digital evidence of narcotics when he searched a suspect's computer for digital evidence of child pornography. In this case the officer had acted under the authority of a search warrant that specified a search for evidence related to narcotics trafficking, and noticed a filename that he believed could be related to child pornography.

In a similar case, but with a different ruling, the court in *United States v. Gray* (1999) found that a federal agent did not violate the scope of a search warrant when he seized all of the files on a suspect's computer while looking for evidence of intrusion into a federal computer. During the course of the agent's search for evidence of hacking, several images of child pornography were discovered. The court denied the defendant's motion to have all of the evidence of child pornography excluded because a successful search pursuant to the agent's warrant would have required him to examine every possible location of potential evidence. It was during just such a thorough search that each of the images of child pornography was discovered.

When first examining the aforementioned areas, it is possible that one would believe the only answer would be for law enforcement officers to list every item that could

Search Warrants for Digital Evidence 79

potentially contain digital evidence, and to conduct all searches on site without any seizure of computer hardware. Searches conducted onsite could potentially solve a portion of the problem, but the solution itself develops a larger problem. The technology has been developed to conduct searches of digital evidence on site without damaging the integrity of the evidence, but the storage capacity of today's computer storage mediums would make a search on site an inconvenient task. The proper examination of a computer's hard drive may take from several days to a few weeks. An examination such as this could place an undue burden on both law enforcement and the owner of the computer system. An investigator facing a situation similar to those discussed should attempt to explain to the magistrate issuing the warrant the need to examine the evidence off site.

If a magistrate determines that the seizure of an entire computer could present a problem, then investigators could settle for making an image of the suspect's hard drive. Because an image is a bit-by-bit copy of the original evidence, the use of an image is an acceptable technique. Further, through the use of computer forensics software an imaged copy of a suspect's storage media can be authenticated in such a manner that the trial court could accept the copy as evidence. This situation could potentially arise in cases involving the search of business computers where seizure would result in financial damages to the suspect's entire office. Absent a belief that the entire company is involved in the criminal activity, a seizure of all computers could be considered excessive by a magistrate.

As to listing each item to be seized under a search warrant, law enforcement officers might avoid possible problems by listing all storage mediums that could potentially contain digital evidence. Many in the field of criminal justice believe that the Fourth Amendment will be applied flexibly in cases involving technology, computers and criminal activities (Dillon, Groene, & Hayward, 1998; Carter & Perry, 2004). Indeed, Jacobsen and Greene (2002) state that a law enforcement officer may, in the course of an authorized search, seize and examine a disk regardless of whether its label indicates it does not contain information within the scope of the warrant. The problem with the rationale of Jacobsen and Greene is that the case upon which they base their belief is over ten years old, and understanding of computer-related storage devices would now appear to counter the ruling in that specific case.

Although courts may have to apply flexible interpretations to future cases involving computers, at this time officers must explain the complexities involved in the investigation of high technology crimes, including the nature of digital evidence, to magistrates issuing warrants. Not only will such an explanation provide the magistrate with reasoning for why computer disks may have to be seized, but the explanation could also be used later if the suspect attempts to argue that law enforcement was "fishing" for evidence. An expert could be brought in by law enforcement personnel to explain these issues if the officers themselves are not familiar with how the various storage mediums work.

Another issue that must be considered when examining the search warrant requirement of the Fourth Amendment is whether the judge issuing the search warrant understands precisely what is to be searched. There are few areas of search and seizure where this is more important than in cases involving high technology crimes and digital evidence. This concern is due in part to the fact there are new advances and new terminology being used in the field of computer technology every day. It is extremely important that law enforcement officers who request a warrant ensure that the judge understands what it is the officer will be searching for and what types of information may be discovered. It has even been recommended that a sealed copy of the images used to develop probable cause for the warrant accompany requests for search warrants for child pornography. By sealing the images within an envelope the magistrate can determine whether or not they wish to examine the actual images of child pornography when deciding whether to issue the warrant. This issue becomes even more important in light of recent court decisions requiring that images of child pornography actually depict children engaged in sexual activity, and not depict adults pretending to be children (Kreston, 2004). Law enforcement officers who do not take this advice risk having their evidence excluded, notwithstanding other acceptable exceptions, such as the good faith clause. Good faith is an acceptable argument when it is determined that the officers were acting under what they reasonably felt was a valid search warrant. To combat these types of circumstances Clark and Diliberto (1996) go so far as to recommend that all officers requesting a search warrant involving computers or other high technology devices carry a pocket dictionary of computer terms and definitions.

Assembling a Search Warrant Team for Computers

As technology assisted crimes continue to increase in frequency, some law enforcement agencies may opt to form a special unit to handle the execution of search warrants involving digital evidence. The need for such a unit is debatable, but one should never fear opting on the side of caution and preparation. Operating in much the same manner as a high-risk warrant execution team, a search warrant team trained for the execution of search warrants involving digital evidence ensures quick and accurate seizure of evidence from computers and other technological devices. Perhaps the best argument against the use of search warrant teams is the cost of assembling a team of individuals capable of handling digital crime scenes, and then balancing this cost with the number of technology-assisted crimes, the agency will investigate. Agencies that operate in small communities might well find themselves unable to justify the formation of such a team. However, agencies in larger cities should seriously consider forming search warrant teams, as the near future is sure to hold more technology crime investigations for state and local law enforcement agencies.

The formation of a search warrant team is important, if for no other reason than the potential for mishandling of digital evidence. With few technology-assisted crimes leaving physical evidence, the mishandling of digital evidence could result in the forfeiture of a case. Law enforcement agencies that do decide to institute a search warrant team are encouraged to follow the guidelines developed by Clark and Diliberto (1996). The team is made up as follows: case supervisor, interview team, sketch and photo team, physical search team, security and arrest team and a technical evidence seizure and logging team. All new personnel is not required, as law enforcement officers outside of the actual high technology crime unit can staff several portions of the team.

The case supervisor is the chief administrative officer of the team and responsible for overseeing the day-to-day operations of the investigative team. Along with being responsible for assembling the team and providing reports to higher administration, the case supervisor is also responsible for annual budgeting, scheduling, and the conducting of the execution of a search warrant; this individual coordinates the execution of the search warrant (Clark & Diliberto, 1996). Case supervisors do not necessarily have to have extensive training in the area of computer forensics, but they should be experienced in the execution of search warrants.

The interview team normally consists of a minimum of one person who is skilled in interrogations, and is responsible for assembling witnesses and or suspects at the scene of the search warrant's execution. Once assembled, this group of team members will conduct interviews with witnesses or suspects. Much like the case supervisor, there is little need for members of the interview team to have extensive training in the area of computer forensics. However, such training could assist the team in formulating the types of questions to be asked of the witnesses and suspects (Clark & Diliberto, 1996). The members of this team, though, must have extensive training in statement analysis and interrogation techniques in order to ensure that the most accurate information is obtained by those at the scene of the search warrant's execution.

The sketch and photo team is responsible for recording on video, or log by photograph, the area of the crime scene both before and after a search warrant is served. This team is important because the pictures and video may be necessary if the case goes to court and the suspect argues that evidence was planted at the scene of the search warrant by investigators on the scene (Clark & Diliberto, 1996).

The physical search team is responsible for identifying and marking all evidence discovered at the crime scene. It is recommended that color-coded sticky dots be used during the marking phase for two reasons. First, coding assists investigators in identifying evidence that does not contribute to the case. Second, computerized equipment can be more easily reassembled if the wires are color-coded. The members of the physical search team need only enough training to assure a thorough search of computer evidence conforming to search-and-seizure law, and the team can be staffed by personnel drawn from other units (Clark & Diliberto, 1996).

The members of the security and arrest team are normally made up of uniformed police officers. The primary responsibility of this team is to provide security of the area surrounding the crime scene in which the warrant is served, and its members assist in the arrest of suspects at the scene. Such duties require no specialized training in computers, and because these individuals are normally uniformed officers. Therefore, team members can be any uniformed officers who are trained security and arrest techniques (Clark & Diliberto, 1996).

The members of the technical evidence seizure and logging team are the most highly trained within the search warrant team. This team, which Clark and Diliberto (1996) recommend maintain at least two or more individuals, is responsible for the safe seizure of the suspect's computer or any other relevant digital evidence. The ideal make-up of this team is a minimum of one computer investigator, who provides information on the proper procedures to follow, and one computer professional, who provides information on the proper methods of disassembling the computer.

At first glance, the size of the search warrant team appears quite large. However, the majority of the team can be drawn from other units. In fact, the only necessary full-time positions are those that require special training and technical certification: the case supervisor and the two members of the technical evidence seizure and tagging team. Hence, a search warrant team can be staffed at relatively small costs.

Executing the Search Warrant

In recent years, several guides providing procedures for executing search warrants involving computers and digital evidence have been published. Many of these guides are very basic introductions to the field of computers and crime and provide nothing more than a simplified series of steps to handle seizing a computer or other technological device. Some of these guides are published by federal law enforcement agencies such as the Secret Service, and some guides are produced by state law enforcement agencies. All of the guides provide information concerning the various types of computerized accessories an officer is likely to encounter on a digital crime scene, and offer information on the execution of a search warrant for digital evidence. In every case, however, the information provided could be considered incomplete. The following discussion is based upon a compilation of recommendations from the various professional search and seizure guides, as well as the author's experience in dealing with computers.

All search and seizure guides agree that the first step in executing a search warrant is to get the suspect away from the computer, and thereby safeguard potential evidence. The removal of the suspect from the computer is vital because of the potential presence of a data-removal program that can be activated with the press of a single key designed to activate the deletion program. This key is sometimes referred to as a hot key. According to Wang (2001), there are innumerable programs available on the Internet that will allow this type of quick destruction of evidence. Even more disconcerting is the fact that the majority of these programs are available at no charge. To control for this type of program, it is imperative that officers move a suspect away from a computer as soon as possible after officers have entered the room.

There are two methods of getting a suspect away from a computer. The first involves the use of a no-knock warrant, which allows for officers executing a warrant to enter the scene without first knocking and alerting a suspect to their presence. There is a potential problem in the use of this technique, as the use of force creates the potential for an excessive force claim. Additionally, magistrates have historically only granted no-knock warrants in extreme cases where there is a potential for evidence to be destroyed quickly and easily. Of course, the volatile nature of computer data could impact a magistrate's decision to grant such a warrant in an extreme case, and in fact some scholars believe that the courts will issue more no-knock warrants for digital evidence in the near future (Bohn & Muster, 2003). Law enforcement officers who pursue this method must ensure that the magistrate understands both the need for the protection of the digital evidence and the exigency involved in executing the search.

Should the use of a no-knock warrant be deemed unacceptable, then a second method of getting a suspect away from a computer is to simply knock on the door, and once the suspect opens the door, the officer has the responsibility of preventing him or her from returning to the computer. There are several different methods of ensuring that the suspect does not return to the computer, but perhaps the easiest way to do this is for the officer in charge to offer a handshake; few people will refuse an offered handshake. Once the handshake is in progress, the officer can lead the suspect away from the computer. Occasionally, the execution of a search warrant for digital evidence may require that executing officers use a combination of gentlemanly behavior and forceful methods. Regardless of the method employed, force must be used if a suspect attempts to regain access to the computer or technological device.

Kruse and Heiser (2002) recommend the entire room be photographed. This is a common practice to prove law enforcement officers executing the search warrant did not plant any false evidence or rearrange the search area. A still camera could be used; however, advances in digital cameras now make these devices a preferable option. If a mistake is made, or if an officer determines that a picture is insufficient then they can see this at the scene and take additional photographs as needed. Advances in camcorder technology have also resulted in a situation where the entire search can be recorded whenever possible. The use of digital camcorders can provide evidence of each step in the search as it actually happens.

Even if the search is being videotaped, the screen of the suspect computer should be photographed exactly as it appears when the officers arrive. If the monitor is off then the officer should turn on the monitor and photograph the screen. If the actual CPU, central processing unit, is off then the computer should be left off and only turned back on by a computer specialist (Kruse & Heiser, 2002).

From the point where the cameras begin filming, all actions in the search should be noted in a detailed search log. Information such as the time of any action involving the computer or other technological device in the search area must be logged into this record. Other notes that should be included involve answers to questions like why the device was touched. This log and its accompanying notes may become necessary to assist the investigating officer in the future should the officer be asked to recall why interactions took place. Should the monitor have to be turned on, the lead officer should make a note in the search log indicating why the monitor was turned on and what was on the screen when it was activated.

The next step is to locate and unhook any phone connections or network connections. The search for network connections on personal computers has become important in recent years because of recent advances in the field of computer networking. Today, it is easier and more affordable to maintain home networks. The danger of a network lies in the fact that any computer connected to the network can control the files and programs on any other computer connected to the same network. It should be noted that this statement is made as a means of providing a general statement. There are numerous methods of controlling the access to other files that are stored on a network; however, explanation of these techniques would exceed the purpose of this work. Here the discussion focuses on how to prevent others from deleting files before the information is seized by law enforcement officers. In order to prevent possible deletion of files or damage to evidence, it is important to disconnect any network cables from the back of the computer.

Like a network connection, there are now programs that allow someone to control another computer over the phone line. Therefore, it is just as important to check for any type of modem connection. Anytime a cable is removed from the back of the computer, a colored label should be placed on the cable removed, and in the area where the cable was removed, thereby facilitating the reconnection of the cables when the computer is reassembled and restarted. It may not seem like much of a problem when the investigation involves one computer, but should the investigation lead to the seizure of two or more computers, the labeling of the cables will aid in the reassembly process. If more than one computer is seized, the labels should be color coordinated and numbered (Mandia & Prosise, 2001). Once again, any labeling must be noted in the search log, along with the type of connection found - network or modem.

The next step in the execution of the warrant is to close out any programs that are running in RAM, which stands for Random Access Memory. These are files currently opened that have not been saved to the hard drive or any other storage media. In Windows operating systems, the files open in RAM can be located by looking at the bottom of the screen. Normally, each individual screen displayed at the bottom of the Windows screen represents a file that is active and stored in RAM. Should the power be cut before the files are taken out of RAM and saved to a disk, then the data can be lost forever. This is the first instance in which the issue of an operating system arises. Each operating system handles files differently and therefore determines how an investigator will be forced to look for the files that are currently open and running in RAM.

If investigators see that there are programs running in the task bar of a Windows computer, they should photograph each of the programs after they are enlarged. Once the files are photographed, they should be saved by the investigator to a floppy disk and given a name that can be associated with the investigation. An example would be to name an opened file "investigation1.doc". Once the file is saved, the investigator must make a notation in the search log indicating the time saved and the file name associated, and provide a brief description of the file. These notes will become very important should the case go to trial. Defense attorneys who specialize in cyber crime defense cases are now pushing for more documentation when a search involves a computer, and failure to provide accurate information may be grounds for a dismissal (Baron-Evans, 2003).

If a computer is running UNIX, or any of its variations such as Linux, the files stored in RAM are handled differently. Processes running in UNIX and Linux are hidden in the background. In order to see what is running, the command "ps" must be entered from the command prompt (Mandia & Prosise, 2001). This will list all processes that are currently running on the computer. Once the processes are determined, the steps are the same as that of a Windows operating system. The necessary files must be saved using a familiar file name, and the search log must be completed for future reference by the investigator. As the Linux operating system has gained acceptance, there have been several advances made in the user-friendly quality of the operating system. For example, newer releases of Linux now come with a windows-based, graphical user interface known as Windows X. When an investigator encounters a computer running Linux's Windows X, the files stored in RAM will be displayed at the bottom of the screen just as the files are shown in the Windows Operating System by Microsoft.

At this point it should be noted that outside assistance may become important. For example, if investigators are not familiar with the various types of operating systems, as is the case for agencies that cannot afford to assemble a trained computer seizure team, then a civilian expert may be used. However, law enforcement agencies that choose this option must ensure that the civilian used is monitored throughout the entire search process. Bohn and Muster (2003) argue that the use of a civilian, while many times necessary, may be dangerous because the individual is not trained in techniques associated with executing search warrants. Further, the individual may not be familiar with the law and may conduct too broad a search. By monitoring the civilian at all times these areas of concern can be avoided.

Once the RAM has been emptied, the computer must be powered down. This is one of the more controversial issues in the execution of a search warrant for digital evidence. Some professionals claim that the solution to powering down the computer is to merely unplug the computer's power cable from the back of the computer. While this will work with systems such as Windows, there are many problems associated with doing so with systems like Linux. UNIX and Linux store past commands in their memory, and the command history list does not update until the computer is powered down. If a Linux machine is shut off without the proper power-down procedure, the history records will be lost forever (Mandia & Prosise, 2001). If the suspect's computer is believed to have been used in the production or distribution of child pornography, the history file may not be as important as it would in a hacker case. The decision to merely unplug the computer, then, must be made on a case-by-case basis. Should the decision be made to unplug the computer, the power cord must be removed from the back of the computer, not from the wall. There are devices that allow a user to set up protections on a computer that will damage the computer if the power is cut off from the wall.

Once the computer is powered down, the next step is to disconnect and label the various parts of the computer. Again, as the cables are removed from the computer, they must be color-coded and labeled to help facilitate the reassembly of the computer at the computer forensics lab (National Institute of Justice, 2001). Notes must be made concerning the various parts of the computer that are disconnected and packaged. There are numerous reasons for the creation of notes, but once again the most important reason for the notes is to assist the investigator should the case go to court and the investigator be forced to testify. The computer is normally the main item listed in the search warrant. Usually, however, other important evidence surrounds the computer. Therefore, consideration must be given to other types of likely evidence, and it should be listed in the search warrant as well. Any well-drafted search warrant includes provisions for the seizure of any floppy disks, CD-ROMs, and DVD-ROMs. Clark and Diliberto (1996) also recommend the collection of manuals that are lying around the computer, as well as technical printouts, since these items can aid investigators in determining (1) which operating systems and programs are running and (2) how to circumvent the software. Along with these manuals, many individuals may leave passwords that will assist in opening files during the investigation. The location of these passwords can range from under the keyboard to under the monitor. Another potential place for criminals to hide evidence or passwords is the inside of the CPU casing.

Once all necessary evidence has been collected, a chain of custody form must be developed (Kruse & Heiser, 2001). The chain of custody form is a listing of all evidence seized from the crime scene and of those investigators who collected the evidence. Once the seizure is completed, all evidence must be taken back and listed on the return sheet. Once the evidence leaves the crime scene, the chain of custody form must list all transfers of evidence.

A more difficult scenario develops in cases where a computer cannot be seized. This scenario unfolds if a computer belonging to a business and playing a key role in the day-to-day operations of the company is involved, yet the business is not able to identify who used the computer during the time the crime occurred, or if the individual used the computer without company permission. When confronted with a scenario similar to this, Brenner and Frederiksen (2002) recommend that investigators ask themselves the following question – was the computer hardware used in the commission of the crime, or is the computer merely the repository of evidence? If the hardware was not used in the crime, then there is little need to seize all of the hardware.

If law enforcement officers are forced to conduct a search onsite, there are two methods of conducting such a search. The first method involves the officer merely conducting a cursory examination of the suspect media for evidence related to the search warrant. If this option is chosen then the officer should ensure that the entire process is videotaped and an accurate log must be maintained. The problem with this approach is that the date and time stamps associated with files may be modified during a search of an active system. Thankfully, there are now computer forensics programs that allow forensic examination of live media without modifying the system. However, some of these programs are very expensive and not all agencies can afford the tools. Use of the videotape will assist in authenticating the search should a skilled trial attorney attempt to argue that the search damaged the integrity of evidence (Kruse & Heiser, 2001). Another problem with an officer conducting the search onsite involves the size of hard drives today. Because an average hard drive is now around 40 gigabytes or more, even cursory onsite searches may be very time consuming for law enforcement officers.

The second method of conducting an onsite search involves making an image of the data onsite. This is a relatively new consideration, as previous technology did not allow for the imaging of a suspect's hard drive without considerable effort. Most computer forensics applications work by connecting a kit hard drive to the suspect hard drive. A kit hard drive is merely a hard drive stored inside of a rugged travel kit. This kit comes with connectors that allows for the copying of data from a suspect hard drive to the kit hard drive. The kit hard drive is then installed within a computer forensics lab computer and the drive is searched for evidence.

Because of the effort it takes to break down the computer and gain access to the internal components, this method is reserved for those who are highly trained in the field of computer technology. There is at least one computer forensics application that has solved the problems associated with taking apart the suspect computer. Recent releases of the EnCase computer forensics software by Guidance Software allows for the kit hard drive to copy the suspect hard drive through the serial port of the suspect computer (Patzakis, 2002). This removes the requirement of disassembling the computer and allows for individuals with less technical computer skill but more training in the use of the computer forensics application to make an image of a hard drive. Baron-Evans and Murphy (2003) have argued that the use of imaging devices are fast and accurate methods of imaging a suspect drive, that can be used in lieu of seizing the compute.

The most desirable method of handling a digital crime scene would be to seize the computer. The company's loss could be minimized if the computer is taken from the scene of the crime for only a short time. Once the computer arrives at the computer forensics lab, the data is transferred to another disk. Once law enforcement personnel are in possession of an accurate copy of the computer's data, and the copy has been verified, then the computer can be returned to the place of business. This approach could be executed in a rather swift and expeditious manner minimizing inconvenience to the owner of the computer system.

The proper drafting and execution of a search warrant for digital evidence is crucial in ensuring that the digital evidence seized from a suspect's computer is both properly obtained and properly stored. Failure to adequately cover both areas may result in the seizure of digital evidence that is later destroyed before trial. Inversely, the data may be secure at the time of the trial, but may be excluded from trial because the evidence was seized outside the confines of the Fourth Amendment and its warrant requirement.

CHAPTER IV

Warrantless Searches and Seizures of Digital Evidence

It has been previously stated that the best method for ensuring a search and seizure is not unreasonable, and therefore not in violation of the Fourth Amendment, is to obtain a properly drafted search warrant. The courts have long agreed that to allow law enforcement officers to search a residence or seize evidence in the absence of a search warrant would leave an individual's privacy and security to the discretion to these same law enforcement officers (*Johnson v. United States*, 1948). When the *Johnson* decision was handed down, there were few in the criminal justice field willing to place their faith in the honesty of law enforcement personnel. This view is still held by many, but there is currently a belief that under certain circumstances a warrantless search may be justified (*United States v. Burns*, 1994).[2] Should law enforcement personnel attempt to argue for the use of a warrantless

---

[2] *United States v. Burns*, 37 F.3d 276 (7th Cir. 1994) – here, the defendant argued her seizure during execution of a search warrant was in violation of the Fourth Amendment. The court, however, in referring to previous Supreme Court decisions, determined that the seizure of the defendant was reasonable because there was a valid search warrant issued and the detention was substantially less intrusive than that of an arrest.

search and seizure, then the government is faced with the task of proving that circumstances justified the excuse of the warrant requirement (*Parkhurst v. Trapp*, 1996).[3] It should be noted that the Supreme Court has only accepted a few exceptions to the requirement for a search warrant. The following section will briefly outline several of these exceptions.

Warrantless Search Doctrines Applied to Physical Evidence

One of the earliest warrantless search doctrines to be accepted by the Supreme Court was that of a search incident to a lawful arrest (*Preston v. United States*, 1964).[4] In considering this doctrine, the most important consideration is that of the arrest. If an officer attempts to make a warrantless search on the basis of an illegal arrest, the evidence will be considered to have been seized outside the Fourth Amendment and will not be admissible in trial. The majority of decisions handed down concerning

---

[3] *Parkhurst v. Trapp*, 77 F.3d 707 (3rd Cir. 1996) – three law enforcement officers searched a suspect's home without a search warrant, and in the absence of the suspect. The court determined there were no exigent circumstances and that the government bore the responsibility of proving there was justification for a warrantless search.

[4] *Preston v. United States*, 376 U.S. 364, 84 S. Ct. 881, 11 L. Ed. 2d 777 (1964) – defendants were arrested outside of a bank on vagrancy charges resulting from sitting in a parked automobile. The car was removed to a garage and later searched without a warrant. The Supreme Court unanimously held that the evidence obtained from the car was inadmissible because the warrantless search was too far removed from the actual arrest and seizure of the automobile. As such, the incident to arrest doctrine was inadmissible and the officers had reasonable time to obtain a search warrant and failed to do so.

warrantless searches incident to a lawful arrest have found justification in this warrantless search doctrine by arguing that its use protects law enforcement officers. For example, if an officer makes an arrest and fails to search the surrounding area, there is the possibility the suspect could escape and cause the officer harm by obtaining a weapon.

Search incident to arrest has been justified on the basis of officer safety, however, weapons are not the only items justified under this warrantless search doctrine. Also in debate is the issue of to what extent a search incident to an arrest is extended. As of today, there is support for allowing the seizure of any destructible evidence found during a search incident to an arrest (*United States v. Bizier*, 1997)[5]; the question currently being considered is whether search incident to a lawful arrest allows for searches beyond the room in which the arrest takes place. In *Chimel v. California* (1969), the United States Supreme Court held that searches could not extend beyond the room in which the arrest was executed. Today, however, there is an increased possibility of weapons being stored in adjacent rooms. With this in mind, the extension of this search doctrine is certain to be tested in the near future.

Another warrantless search doctrine, one that is often discussed when considering searches incident to an arrest, is that of exigent circumstances. The foundation for this

---

[5] *United States v. Bizier*, 111 F.3d 214 (1st Cir. 1997) – defendant and a friend were pulled over for speeding. The officers were alerted that the individual was under investigation for sale of narcotics (on the basis of information obtained from an informant). After removing the individuals from the car, the defendant granted consent to search the vehicle. After searching the vehicle, officers found narcotics on the defendant's person. The court found that the search incident to arrest doctrine not only applies to searches for weapons, but also to searches involving the protection of evidence.

doctrine dates back several decades (*Warden v. Hayden*, 1967)[6], and is used by the law enforcement officers to justify searches that are conducted in situations where obtaining a search warrant would result in one of the following: (1) life is threatened, (2) a suspect's escape is imminent, or (3) evidence is about to be destroyed (*United States v. Ball*, 1996).[7] Several common examples of exigent circumstances are hot pursuit, a fleeing suspect, destruction of evidence or other situations in which speed is essential (Hermann, 1998). Exigent circumstances often impact cases involving searches incident to an arrest because of reason number one above, and reason number three above. Most searches incident to a lawful arrest are conducted to protect the lives of officers making the arrest, or to protect evidence that could be damaged by the suspect.

Not all warrantless search doctrines require the absence of a search warrant. There are situations in which law

---

[6] *Warden v. Hayden*, 387 U.S. 294, 87 S. Ct. 1642, 18 L. Ed. 2d 782 (1967) – defendant was arrested after law enforcement officers arrived at his home and conducted a warrantless search on the basis of information leading them to believe that a person who had committed a robbery had entered the home a few minutes prior. The Supreme Court ruled that the evidence obtained during the search was admissible for several reasons, but the most applicable to the discussion at hand was the reasoning that the circumstances of the case and the exigencies of the situation made the search imperative.

[7] *United States v. Ball*, 90 F.3d 260 (8th Cir. 1996) – defendant was arrested after an informant provided law enforcement with information relating to the presence of narcotics and firearms at the defendant's residence. Upon arriving at the scene, the defendant fled into the house. Upon following the defendant in, drug paraphernalia was discovered. The court found that exigent circumstances exist in situations where the three aforementioned conditions are met.

enforcement officers are executing a search warrant and discover additional evidence that is not listed on their search warrant. Under the plain view exception to the warrant requirement, additional evidence can be seized if certain conditions are met. First, the incriminating nature of the evidence must be apparent without being touched by law enforcement officers. If an item is moved before law enforcement officers are able to articulate its illegality, the evidence cannot be seized. Second, the officer must be in a place where he or she has a lawful right to be. Here, there is no problem if an officer is executing a search warrant. Should the officer enter a residence without a warrant or permission, though, all evidence seized under the plain view doctrine is inadmissible, barring some other warrantless search exception that justifies the entrance into the home (*United States v. Bradshaw*, 1996).[8]

Searches conducted incident to an arrest and under the plain view doctrine are commonplace, but perhaps the greatest warrantless search exception is that of consent to nullify the requirement of a search warrant. Consent merely means that the suspect grants the law enforcement officer permission to conduct a search without a search warrant. There are several problems, however, with the use of consent doctrine, the greatest being the ability of the

---

[8] *United States v. Bradshaw*, 102 F.3d 204 (6th Cir. 1996) – during a traffic stop, law enforcement personnel discovered the presence of narcotics lying on the seat beside the defendant. Upon reaching in to seize the evidence, the officer noticed a handgun sticking out from the seat. The defendant attempted to argue that the plain view doctrine did not apply because the stop was inappropriate. The court found that the stop was valid and therefore the plain view search was acceptable. The court did imply that had the officer had no reason for the stop then the search would have been invalid because the officer was not in a place he maintained a legal right to be.

suspect to withdraw his or her consent. This could become an issue not only during the search, but after the search as well. Consider the following: a suspect could grant an officer permission to search his or her residence. Upon the officer finding some form of contraband and arresting the suspect, the individual could argue that they never granted consent to search their residence. For this reason, the courts have generally held that the government bears the burden of proving that the suspect did in fact grant consent and understood to what the consent related (*Bumper v. North Carolina*, 1968).[9]

Of course, an officer who believes there is the possibility of having their consent to search challenged could respond appropriately to ensure that the consent is documented. Documentation, however, does not always solve the problem, as the suspect may withdraw their consent without verbally informing the officer of the withdrawal of their consent. The withdrawal of consent is a complicated topic, and is one that warrants an essential discussion. Another question recently challenged before the United States Supreme Court is whether law enforcement officers are required to inform suspects of their right to refuse consent. It was the opinion of the Supreme Court that it would be unreasonable to always require a law enforcement officer to inform a suspect of their right to refuse a consent

---

[9] *Bumper v. North Carolina*, 391 U.S. 543, 88 S. Ct. 1788, 20 L. Ed. 2d 797 (1968) – the defendant was convicted of rape. During trial he argued that evidence introduced in trial was obtained illegally because his grandmother granted consent. The Supreme Court found that the grandmother could have granted consent but the government failed to prove that law enforcement had proved the grandmother understood her consent and her right to refuse. In fact, the officers informed the grandmother that they were in possession of a search warrant and therefore did not need her consent.

search. In the opinion of the court, a totality of the circumstances test would be better suited to the use of consent searches (*Ohio v. Robinette*, 1996).[10]

Another issue in the use of consent searches is third-party consent. The term third-party consent is used to describe a search that is not authorized by the suspect of the crime but is authorized by another individual who lives in the residence or has common control over the area to be searched. For example, a wife may grant permission to search a computer that is co-owned by both herself and her spouse. On the other hand, the manager of a hotel cannot grant consent to search a patron's room because allowing such a search would remove constitutional protections from those who would use the services of the hotel (*Stoner v. California*, 1964).[11] It should be noted, however, that at least one court has ruled that officers who relied on an invalid consent did not violate the Fourth Amendment because they were acting in good faith and could not prove

---

[10] *Ohio v. Robinette*, 519 U.S. 33, 117 S. Ct. 417, 136 L. Ed. 2d 347 (1996) – law enforcement officers stopped defendant for speeding. After issuing the citation, the officer asked the defendant whether there were any narcotics or weapons in the car. After the defendant responded "no" the officer asked to search the car. Later, the defendant attempted to argue that the search was illegal because he was unaware of his right to refuse consent. The Supreme Court found that an officer does not have to inform a suspect of their "right to go" before obtaining consent.

[11] *Stoner v. California*, 376 U.S. 483, 84 S. Ct. 889, 11 L. Ed. 2d 856 (1964) – defendant was convicted of armed robbery. Several articles were admitted into evidence that were seized from a hotel room with the permission of the hotel clerk. The Supreme Court held unanimously that the search was unlawful because the search was not conducted incident to a lawful arrest and the clerk's consent did not waive the individual's Fourth Amendment protections.

that the consent was invalid (*United States v. Elliot*, 1995).[12]

Application of Warrantless Search Doctrines to the Seizure of Digital Evidence

Currently, there are few court decisions that relate to technology crimes, but there are several decisions that could be considered as a foundation for future decisions. The United States Supreme Court has generally held that a person maintains a reasonable expectation to privacy in closed containers (*United States v. Ross*, 1982).[13] Because of this idea, it has been recommended by Orin Kerr (2001) of the Computer Crime and Intellectual Property Section of the Department of Justice that it is best to treat the computer as a briefcase or special filing cabinet. Since the Fourth Amendment would generally, but not always, prevent the search and seizure of these types of items, it

---

[12] *United States v. Elliot*, 50 F.3d 180 (2d Cir. 1995) – law enforcement officers conducted a search on the basis of consent. Later, it was determined that the individual in question did not have the necessary control over the area to validate the consent. The court, however, ruled that the officers were acting under good faith and therefore the search was validated.

[13] *United States v. Ross*, 456 U.S. 798, 102 S. Ct. 2157, 72 L. Ed. 2d 572 (1982) – law enforcement officers, working on information obtained from a confidential informant, stopped a vehicle and arrested the occupants after a brown paper bag in the trunk was determined to be narcotics. The vehicle was taken to headquarters and searched again, at which time a zippered pouch was opened. The defendant claimed the evidence was seized illegally because there was no search warrant for opening closed containers. The Supreme Court ruled that after a vehicle is stopped, if officers have probable cause to believe there is contraband, then a search might be as thorough as a magistrate could authorize. This includes searches of containers.

would be best for law enforcement officers to obtain a warrant unless the situation falls under another warrant exception.

Several court decisions have held that a computer's hard drive is exactly comparable to a filing cabinet and must therefore be treated in the same manner (*United States v. Barth*, 1998).[14] The case of *United States v. Blas* (1990)[15] provides clearer proof that the courts have found technological devices to be similar to containers. In the *Blas* decision, the judges stated that a computer, a pager, or any similar device must be treated in a manner comparable to that of a "closed container".

There are times when a closed container can be opened without a warrant. Should the information contained in the computer, briefcase, or filing cabinet be viewable by the public, then the owner of the information has waived his

---

[14] *United States v. Barth*, 26 F.Supp.2d 929 (1998) – defendant was arrested for possession of child pornography after his computer repairman noticed images during a repair and notified law enforcement officers. It was the opinion of the court that the repairman was not a state actor when the initial images were discovered. Subsequent images that were discovered after law enforcement was notified were not admissible because at this point the repairman became an actor under state law.

[15] *United States v. Blas*, 1990 U.S. Dist. LEXIS 19961 (E.D. Wis. 1990) – Upon suspect's exiting of a vehicle, an officer asked to examine suspect's pager. After obtaining the pager, the officer then searched through the device and wrote down several numbers that he later used to make further arrests. The court found that the officer's permission to examine the pager did not include consent to examine the contents of the pager. As such, the evidence obtained from the illegal search was barred from admission at trial.

right to privacy (*United States v. David*, 1991).[16] Another way a computer and its contents can be considered public and not private is if the information is stored on a stolen computer or other stolen technological device (*United States v. Lyons*, 1993).[17]

Reasonable Expectation of Privacy

Even if an individual maintains a reasonable expectation of privacy in a technological storage device, there are situations in which the individual may lose this right to privacy. When an individual turns over control of an item to a third party, he or she may lose their reasonable expectation of privacy. An example of how this can be applied to technology would be the known drug dealer who ships a laptop, which is believed to contain buyer information, to an associate operating under a known alias. The fact that the individual is operating under an assumed

---

[16] *United States v. David*, 756 F. Supp. 1385 (D. Nev. 1991) – law enforcement officers seized a data book and obtained information from the computer after law enforcement officers feared the suspect was deleting information. The password to the device was obtained when an officer looked over the shoulder of the suspect as he typed. The court found that the password was not illegally obtained, as the officer was where he was allowed to be and the suspect brought forth the information for all to see. The seizure of the data book was held to be acceptable because of exigency in protecting data. The search, however, was found to be invalid because exigency ended upon the seizure of the device.

[17] *United States v. Lyons*, 992 F.2d 1029 (10th Cir. 1993) – defendant was arrested and charged with the theft of computer related equipment. Upon his arrest, the computer parts were seized and searched. The defendant argued that his Fourth Amendment privacy rights had been violated, but the court disagreed finding that there is no expectation of privacy in stolen goods.

name could potentially allow law enforcement to seize the evidence or conduct a search.

An individual's loss of control over information can become especially important in dealing with issues such as posting of information in chat rooms. In the case of *United States v. Charbonneau* (1997), the court reasoned that a defendant did not retain his reasonable expectation of privacy in information that he posted to an America Online chat room. It was the Court's belief that information posted in chat rooms cannot be considered private because there is no way for the individual to verify who is on the other end of the computers receiving the postings. Because the courts have long held that information told to undercover law enforcement officers does not maintain any right of privacy, the court felt that there could be no way that an individual posting to a chat room could discover whether the individuals receiving the postings are undercover officers.

A related issue, which has yet to be fully addressed by the courts, is whether the Internet is public or private. Seeger and Visconte (1997) coined the term "Privlic" because the Internet and chat rooms can be viewed from the privacy of one's home where a reasonable expectation of privacy does exist, but the information is also viewable by anyone who is connected to the Internet. The issue in *Charbonneau*, however, was focused on postings to chat rooms and not on the issue of electronic mail messages. E-mails are still regulated by the Electronic Communications Privacy Act of 1986, which controls who may obtain electronic communications and the legal process required for such an action. Therefore, in order to obtain an unread e-mail an investigator will usually have to obtain a search warrant.

Investigators seizing e-mail, then, should acquire a search warrant. There are, however, exceptions granted by the

Electronics Communication Privacy Act and by other statutes as well. The first exception would be the "false-friend" doctrine. Under this doctrine, a person cannot maintain a reasonable expectation of privacy in information that has been conveyed to a third party. Therefore, an investigator who obtains e-mail from an individual who received e-mail from a suspect does not have to have a search warrant to read the e-mail (Seeger & Visconte, 1997).

The next method of obtaining an individual's e-mail is through the Internet service provider. The Electronic Communications Privacy Act of 1986 (ECPA) provides that no one may **intercept** electronic communications while being transmitted on a public system. There is no stipulation in the ECPA saying that, once the electronic mail is deposited within an Internet service provider's (ISP) main server, the ISP cannot turn over e-mails to law enforcement agencies. In fact, it has been generally held that owners maintain a diminished expectation of privacy in e-mails because they are stored on an ISP's server (Ko, 2004). There are, however, rules regarding this, and the most important rule would be that in order for an ISP to turn over e-mails or transactional information, the ISP administrator must not have previously contacted law enforcement. Once law enforcement has been contacted, the ISP administrator is considered an agent of the state, and in order for law enforcement to obtain transactional records the use of an "articulable facts" court order becomes necessary. The case of *United States v. Hambrick* (1999)[18] held that customers of Internet Service Providers

---

[18] *United States v. Hambrick*, 55 F.Supp.2d 504 (W.D. Va. 1999) – defendant was arrested and charged with enticing a fourteen year old boy to come live with him. Law enforcement obtained the defendant's

do not have a reasonable expectation of privacy in customer account records maintained by the provider's business.

If the idea of e-mail being stored in the ISP's computer is confusing, then one must understand that even after an e-mail is deleted off an individual's computer, there is still a copy remaining in every e-mail server that the message passed through. Therefore, as e-mail is transferred from one ISP to another, multiple copies are made. This was originally used as a protection against lost information or computer failure. Now however, it has lead to debates concerning the accessibility of e-mail.

The Federal Bureau of Investigation recently faced controversy when it attempted to introduce its new e-mail-sniffing program, DCS1000, which is perhaps better known by its original name, Carnivore. The program was named Carnivore for its ability to sniff out the meat of e-mail headers and web site addresses. Once installed on an Internet Service Provider's main server, the Carnivore program monitors e-mails and web usage that contains key words or phrases. When the program determines that a user has entered one of the key words, a copy of the e-mail or web page information is copied into a file that is later viewed by agents of the FBI. The problem the FBI is currently facing is a lack of cooperation by ISPs. Many Internet providers believe that to allow the installation of

---

identity through his Internet Service Provider on the basis of a subpoena, which was later found to be invalid. The court ruled that the information provided to the defendant was allowable under the Electronics Communications Privacy Act. Further, the court commented on the lack of direction by congress when ECPA was written in regards to the admission of evidence seized outside ECPA. According to the court in the case at hand, evidence seized illegally may still be entered into evidence.

the Carnivore program would violate their subscribers' privacy (Seeger & Visconte, 1997). Thanks to the recent passage of the USA PATRIOT Act, this issue may be less debatable in the future.

The passage of the USA PATRIOT Act may seriously influence the course of a debate that raged several years ago when Earthlink Communications challenged the installation of Carnivore in court. The judge determined that an ISP had a right to refuse installation of Carnivore, so long as there was a suitable alternate program capable of performing a similar function installed. With this in mind, Earthlink introduced its own program entitled Altivore, which differed from Carnivore in that only e-mails of suspects were copied (Seeger & Visconte, 1997).

For one of Earthlink's customers to be placed within the scope of the Altivore program, law enforcement agents were required to present the company with a search warrant. Earthlink would then input the suspect's name into the program and forward any evidence that was uncovered to the proper authorities. After the passage of the USA PATRIOT Act, the requirements for such warrants are now considered to be non-stringent. Once permission is granted for a warrant, then all of a suspect's communication devices can be tapped. Warrants that fall into this category are commonly referred to as roving wiretaps, which means that the warrant covers home phones, office phones, cellular phones, fax communications, and electronic communications. It will be interesting to see whether future attempts to challenge the use of DCS1000, the less intimidating name for Carnivore, will be impacted by the passage of the USA PATRIOT Act.

An additional method of circumventing the Electronic Communication Protection Act involves law enforcement obtaining e-mail from a business that suspects one of its employees of criminal activity. It is conservatively estimated that approximately 45% of all employers monitor their employee's e-mail (Estrella, 2001). Unlike ISPs, a business has the right to access the personal e-mail of their employees regardless of reason, as long as the e-mail is sent or received from a company computer, even if the company maintains a written policy stating that it will not monitor employee e-mail (*Alana Shears v. Epson America Inc.*, 1994).[19]

Tied to this issue is the Freedom of Information Act. Should an individual guilty of a crime, or suspected of a crime, use a computer that falls under government use jurisdiction then the individual's e-mails can be made public. This procedure has been most notably used in recent years in the trials of political and public service official, such as in the case of one of the officers involved in the Rodney King affair, who had e-mails where he bragged about his actions used as evidence. This method, while legally acceptable, is a rarely used method (Freedom of Information Act, 1966; Ginden, 1999).

In many circumstances, none of the above exceptions will be available to law enforcement officers. In cases such as this, it is still possible to get some information on a suspect without a warrant, but there are stringent guidelines. Under the Electronics Communication Privacy Act of 1986, certain information can be obtained using a subpoena or a

---

[19] *Alana Shears v. Epson America Inc.,* 1994 Cal. Lexis 3670 (1994) – here, defendant argued that her right to privacy was violated when her e-mail account was monitored. At issue was the policy of the company to not monitor e-mail use. The court ruled that a company maintained the right to monitor the use of its equipment (including e-mail and computers) regardless of whether they maintained a policy against such activities.

court order.[20] A subpoena is required to obtain basic subscriber information as described in Section 2703(c)(1)(C), which is information relating to the name of the subscriber, the subscriber's address, local and long distance billing records, telephone number (or other account identifier if the ISP service is not dial up), type of service provided, and length of service rendered by the ISP. A subpoena can also be used to obtain opened e-mails, unopened e-mails that are greater than 180 days old, or files that are stored on the server of the ISP. Under no circumstances can a subpoena be used to obtain actual e-mail communications that are less than 180 days old.

A court order is required to obtain transactional information as described in Section 2703(c)(1)(B), which is information between the basic subscriber information and the actual content of e-mails, including past audit trail, audit logs, and the addresses of past e-mail correspondents. The order to compel the release of this type of information is known as a section 2703(d) court order or an articulable facts order. The court order is so-named because of the requirement that "specific and articulable facts showing that there are reasonable grounds to believe that the specified records are relevant and material to an ongoing criminal investigation". The obtaining of a 2703(d) court order requires a lower standard than probable cause.

A search warrant is required to obtain and view the actual content information of e-mails stored on an ISP's server. The search warrant is also required to obtain unopened e-mails that are less than 180 days old. A higher-level process will always prevail, meaning that a court order will always be acceptable to obtain subscriber information and a

---

[20] Section 2703 of the Electronics Communication Act of 1986 is provided in full text in Appendix B.

warrant will always be acceptable to obtain transactional information or subscriber information.

Right to Privacy Over Time

According to Orin Kerr (2001), an individual may maintain a reasonable expectation of privacy at one point in time and then lose that right over a period of time. Kerr supports this argument by citing the case of *United States v. Poulsen* (1994). Kevin Poulsen, a hacker discussed earlier in this work, collected numerous pieces of phone company equipment and computers during the process of defrauding several telecommunications companies. Along with several other pieces of evidence, Poulsen kept stolen computers and computer data tapes stored in a rented locker facility.

When Poulsen failed to pay the rent on the facility, the owner of the storage facility entered the storage locker with the intent of removing the belongings. Upon the manager's entering the locker, he immediately noticed an abundance of computer equipment. Because of this discovery, the manager elected to notify both local law enforcement and the phone company whose brand name was on the phone equipment. At Poulsen's trial, he attempted to have the evidence seized from several of the computer tapes removed, with his argument revolving around a belief that the evidence had been illegally seized. The court, however, rejected Poulsen's argument based on their belief that Poulsen's privacy expectation disappeared along with his right to access the facility when he failed to make payment.

Several of the court's past decisions that they perceived to be related to the issue at hand was consulted when making their decision. The first case was *United States v. Haddad* (1977), where the court was asked to determine whether an individual maintained a right to privacy in a hotel room after he failed to pay the rental fee for an additional night. The individual in question failed to make his required payment because he was asked to leave after entering the lobby intoxicated and causing a disturbance. It was the court's opinion that when the defendant was asked to leave, he lost his right to control over the room and as a result lost his privacy in the hotel room.

The case more closely akin to that of *Poulsen* was that of *United States v. Rahme* (1987), where the court was asked to examine whether an individual maintained a right to privacy in a briefcase left in a hotel room after the rental period expired. The court determined that once an individual's allotted time in a specific area was over then their right to privacy within that area, and any contents within that area, were no longer private in the context of a Fourth Amendment search. According to the court, even the expectation to privacy in items like briefcases and luggage did not exist once the allotted time had expired and the owner of the facility had regained control of the room.

It should be noted that when examining the aforementioned cases, it becomes clear that the main issue at stake is the issue of control. Therefore, it should not be stated that time plays the important role, but it is instead the combination of expiring time and the subsequent loss of control of the property that leads to an individual's loss of privacy rights in situations like that of the *Poulsen* case.

Consent Searches

Generally, the courts have held that an individual may grant law enforcement officers the right to search a computer or any other technological device. When dealing with consent to search computers there are several important considerations. First, the individual must have a legitimate right to grant consent; an individual's consent is based upon several factors. Consent must be granted by an individual who is free from duress or coercion and the individual must be capable of understanding that he or she is granting consent to a search that could be used against him or her (*Boyd v. United States* 1886).[21] The Supreme Court further extended the use of consent with their decision in *Schneckloth v. Bustamonte* (1973),[22] which provided that law enforcement personnel do not have to inform a suspect that he or she has a right to refuse consent. Officers must ensure, however, that the individual is old enough and intelligent enough to understand exactly what their agreement covers. A state's courts can tighten this ruling, as several states have expounded on this and required that officers provide suspects with information informing them that they may refuse the consent request. The reasoning for this would appear to be that providing the suspect with information concerning a right to refuse consent assures the courts that the individual is mature

---

[21] *Boyd v. United States*, 116 U.S. 616, 6 S. Ct. 524, 29 L. Ed. 746 (1886) – at issue in here was whether a law requiring a suspect to provide papers as evidence against themselves was invalid under the Fourth Amendment. While some justices felt the issue was more akin to a criminal proceeding under the Fifth Amendment, the court also found that the use of such laws would result in a defendant granting too broad a consent. To use consent the individual must be aware of ability to deny permission.

[22] *Schneckloth v. Bustamonte*, 412 U.S. 218, 93 S. Ct. 2041, 36 L. Ed. 2d 854 (1973) – here defendant was charged with possession of stolen checks. The checks were obtained after an officer stopped the defendant and asked permission to search the car. At trial, the defendant attempted to argue that he was not aware of his right to refuse consent. The Supreme Court found that consent searches should be examined by taking a totality of the circumstances approach. Further, an intelligent and knowing waiver of Fourth Amendment rights is not required.

enough to understand the gravity of the consent in which they are granting.

Particularity is another issue when discussing consent to search technological devices. If the suspect and the investigating officer do not have the same idea, in regard to what items the consent extends to, then the resulting evidence may be excluded. A situation such as the one discussed occurred in the case of *United States v. Blas* (1990), where the court found that the suspect's consent to examine the pager he was carrying did not extend to consent to search the contents of the pager. It was the opinion of the court that the officer's request to examine the pager could reasonably have been construed as a request to examine the pager in an attempt to ensure that the pager was not in fact a weapon.

Returning to the case of *Schneckloth v. Bustamonte* (1973), the court reached a different decision. Here, it was the opinion of the court that the individual's consent to look inside their vehicle was an implied consent for the officer to examine the contents of the pager found within. To avoid confusion when handling cases like that previously discussed, it is recommended that any search that could result in possible confusion be documented with an in depth written consent form completed by the investigating officer and the suspect. The term in depth is used to indicate that the following should be included: (1) the area to be searched, (2) what it is the investigator is intending to search for, and (3) the investigator's desire to search within any computer or technological device found within the area.

Once consent is given then an investigating officer must take care and ensure that he or she does not overstep the bounds of the consent agreement. In *United States v. Carey*

(1999)[23] the court found that an investigating officer overstepped the bounds of his search agreement when he took the suspect's computer off property before he searched it, but after the suspect granted consent to search and seize any property "in his house". This is an important issue for investigators of high technology crimes because of the large-scale storage capabilities of today's computers. As previously discussed, a complete search may not be possible at one sitting onsite, and any consent form to search a computer should indicate the investigating officer's potential need to make an image of the hard drive, or take the computer with him or her for examination. Additionally, it is recommended that an investigator never attempt to seize a computer or other technological device under a consent agreement, because the owner of the property may withdraw a written consent form at any time. Instead, an investigator should invest the time necessary to obtain an adequately drafted search warrant.

The Florida courts have provided what could be considered one of the best examinations of this issue, and have determined that an individual withdraws his or her consent when one or more of the following occurs:

(1) the suspect withdraws consent verbally (*State v. Hammonds*, 1990),[24]

---

[23] *United States v. Carey*, 172 F.3d 1268 (10th Cir. 1999) - Here the court ruled on plain view in regards to digital searches. Officers investigating evidence of an assault encountered evidence of an additional crime while searching a suspect's computer. The investigator then immediately abandoned his search for evidence of assault and began searching for evidence of the new crime. It was the opinion of the court that had the investigator stopped with the initial discovered evidence, the evidence would have been admissible on an application for a search warrant.

(2) the individual withdraws consent through an act such as grabbing the investigator's hand to stop the search of a specific area (*Jimenez v. State*, 1994)[25], or (3) the individual flees during the search (*Davis v. State*, 1986).[26]

One final issue to consider when dealing with high technology crimes and digital evidence is that of third party consent. Bill Gates, founder of Microsoft, has made drastic strides toward an accomplishment that rival Steve Jobs once strove for, the placement of a computer in every

---

[24] *State v. Hammonds*, 557 So. 2d 179 (Fla. 3d DCA 1990) – here the defendant granted law enforcement officers the right to search her two bags of luggage. After searching the first "tote" bag, the defendant began searching the second bag. After the officer indicated he would rather search the bag himself, the defendant said nothing but subsequently indicated she was embarrassed because of undergarments in the bag. The court found the initial search legitimate but found the second garment bag to have been illegally searched. The court did not agree that the defendant's silence granted consent to a search.

[25] *Jimenez v. State*, 643 So. 2d 70 (Fla. 2d DCA 1994) – here an off-duty law enforcement officer discovered cocaine during the conducting of pat-down searches of individuals who attended a dance. The individual initially consented to the search as a condition of entering the building for the dance. During the pat down, however, the officer discovered two cigarette packs. When the officer attempted to search the packs, the individual moved his hand to prevent the officer from finishing the search. The officer completed the search and discovered the cocaine. It was the opinion of the court that the defendant's placing of his hand over the pack was equivalent to withdrawing consent and there was no need for verbal withdrawal.

[26] *Davis v. State*, 497 So. 2d 1344 (Fla. 5d DCA 1986) – law enforcement officers encountered the defendant when the mistook him for a narcotics suspect. While searching the defendant's person, he ran away. When the defendant was caught, he was searched. The court found that the officers had no grounds to detain the defendant and his consent to be searched was revoked when he ran.

home. Because many families and roommates may share a computer, the issue of third party consent could play a potentially serious role in high technology crime investigations and the subsequent searches of personal computers for digital evidence, and such consent has long been held as an acceptable exception to the warrant requirement (*United States v. Matlock*, 1974; *Illinois v. Rodriguez*, 1990).

When examining third-party consent to search technological devices, there are several considerations. Perhaps the most important is whether the individual has the right to grant consent to search the computer in question. In *United States v. Smith* (1998), the court found there was no violation of the Fourth Amendment when law enforcement officers searched a suspect's computer on the basis of consent obtained from the individual's girlfriend. The court based its decision upon the fact that the two individuals lived together and that the suspect had taken no steps to ensure that his files were password protected, thereby making the files accessible by others in the house. Other courts have further ruled that neither ownership nor family relationship can overcome this requirement of access. In *United States v. Durham* (1998), the court found that a mother could not grant consent to the search of a computer, despite the fact that she owned some of the computer equipment. It was the court's belief that the suspect had taken adequate steps to ensure that his mother could not gain access to the computer. The child in question paid a small rental fee to his parents for his room, which was a factor the courts deemed important to the loss of control over the child's belongings. These belongings included the computer in question. Despite the mother owning a portion of the computer, the loss of control over the room rendered the mother's consent invalid.

There is one recent defense to a scenario such as that discussed above. Law enforcement officers who rely on consent of a parent to search a computer within the parent's home may be able to rely on the "apparent authority" doctrine. Under this doctrine a consent search may be ruled admissible even if it is later discovered that the individual granting consent lacked the standing to do so. However, for the search to be ruled valid officers must show that they took reasonable steps to confirm that the individual who granted the consent appeared to have access to the computer and therefore had standing to grant consent to the search (Berg, 2004).

Law enforcement officers who encounter a case involving third party consent should take each of these issues into consideration, in order to ensure the individual granting the consent truly has the authority to grant such consent. If the individual lives in the residence, has access to the room in which the computer is placed, and has access to the data of the computer, then law enforcement officials should not encounter any problems in regards to the validity of the search. The courts, however, have not yet addressed whether a third party may grant consent to search files on a computer if the files are password protected but the password is placed in a place known to the third party. If any of the files are password protected, or if the entire computer is password protected, then a search warrant should be obtained before continuing the search. Regardless of whether the password may be obtainable by a third party, a court could easily view the use of a password as an attempt to ensure privacy from the third party.

Exigent Circumstances

Exigent circumstances have long been held as a means of providing an exception to the warrant requirement, however, to prove exigent circumstances it must be shown that "a reasonable person would believe that entry was necessary to prevent physical harm to the officers or others, the destruction of relevant evidence, the escape of the suspect, or some other consequence that improperly frustrates legitimate law enforcement efforts" (*United States v. Alfonso*, 1985).[27]

The considerations for determining whether a situation meets the requirements of an exigent circumstance seizure were laid out in the case of *United States v. Reed* (1991).[28] The requirements are as follows: (1) degree of urgency, (2) amount of time to obtain warrant, (3) whether the evidence is about to be moved or destroyed, (4) possibility of danger at the scene, (5) whether suspect knows law enforcement is after evidence, and (6) how easy is the evidence to destroy?

It is believed that warrantless seizures justified under exigent circumstances will play a very important role in future technology crime investigations because of the ease in which data can be erased from most technological

---

[27] *United States v. Alfonso*, 759 F.2d 728 (9th Cir. 1985) – defendant was arrested in his hotel room after a search by customs revealed that the ship in which he arrived was loaded with narcotics. The defendant claimed that the search of the hotel was illegal. The court disagreed, finding that law enforcement are allowed to conduct a warrantless search when it becomes apparent that they have probable cause to suspect that evidence may be removed or damaged.

[28] *United States v. Reed*, 15 F.3d 928 (9th Cir. 1994) – believing that quests were acting suspiciously, the manager of a hotel contacted law enforcement and provided them with his concerns. Using the hotel's master key, the manager went into the room. The officer stood in the doorway after entering just far enough to ensure the manager was safe. At this time, the officer merely watched the manager conduct a search. The court denied the government's claim they were the beneficiaries of a private search. Here, the court laid out the circumstances necessary for an exigent circumstance to exist.

storage devices. In *United States v. David* (1991), law enforcement officers seized a suspect's electronic data book after one of the officers realized the suspect was deleting information from the data book. The court agreed that exigent circumstances did in fact exist in the case, as there appeared to be evidence held on the data book that was being deleted. It should be noted that while the court found the deletion of the data created an exigent circumstance and justified the seizure of the data book, they also determine that the exigent circumstances ended when the evidence was seized and the threat of data deletion was no longer present.

In discussing exigent circumstance seizures of digital evidence, the main issue is how likely is the data to be lost if law enforcement were to take the time to obtain a warrant? In the case of *United States v. Ortiz* (1996), the court found there was no Fourth Amendment violation when law enforcement officers searched a pager, retrieved phone numbers and then recorded phone numbers after the arrest of a suspect. The court's reasoning was based on the belief that pagers, and their data, are extremely volatile and subject to being easily deleted or lost if the batteries were to die.

Not all lower courts have agreed with the decision in *Ortiz*. In the case of *United States v. Romero-Garcia* (1997), the court held that a search of a battery operated computer without a search warrant was invalid. The court rejected the law enforcement officer's claim that exigent circumstances were present because of the possibility of lost data should the battery have died. Ultimately, the court determined that unlike a pager that loses its settings and data when the battery is turned off, a computer can maintain its data if the battery dies. When considering this, it is doubtful that an exigency claim to search a computer or laptop could be successfully argued. Law enforcement officers that encounter a suspect who is deleting data should realize they have a right to seize the computer but should not continue their course of action by searching the computer until an adequately prepared search warrant has been drafted.

The recent decision of *Illinois v. McArthur* (2001), has added a new perspective to this area of law by stating that law enforcement officers may prevent a suspect from gaining access to an area that contains potential evidence during the period that another officer is obtaining a search warrant. In the *McArthur* case, the court found that the inconvenience the suspect suffered by not being allowed to return inside his home until a warrant was obtained was outweighed by the potential for the discovery of important evidence. If a court has found that preventing a suspect from entering their home is not unreasonable, then a court should also agree that removing a computer from a suspect's possession until a search warrant is drafted should be acceptable.

Search Incident to an Arrest

It is generally accepted that in order for a search incident to an arrest to be considered lawful, there must be: (1) a lawful arrest, and (2) the search must be contemporaneous with the arrest (*United States v. Moorehead*, 1995).[29]

---

[29] *United States v. Moorehead*, 57 F.3d 875 (1995) – here, the defendant was stopped for speeding. Having no driver's license, the officer ran a background check on the basis of an identification card. The background check revealed there was a warrant for the defendant's arrest. After arresting the defendant, a search of the vehicle turned up a firearm. Being a felon, the defendant was not allowed to be in possession of a firearm. The court found that the search was valid

Further, the Supreme Court ruled in *United States v. Robinson* (1973)[30] that law enforcement officers could search the immediate area of a suspect for the protection and safety of the officer and others in the area. The federal courts extended this concept into the realm of technology and digital evidence with the decision of *United States v. Tank* (2000), where the court's ruling allowed for law enforcement officers to search a zip disk that was taken from the immediate area of a suspect after his arrest. The court, in deciding *Tank,* relied heavily on their prior decision *Illinois v. Lafayette* (1983)[31], where it was ruled that any article or container in an individual's possession during the booking process was subject to a warrantless search.

There are several problems with the reasoning used by the ninth circuit, and as such, individuals involved in the

---

because there was a lawful arrest and the search was contemporaneous with the arrest.

[30] *United States v. Robinson*, 414 U.S. 218, 94 S. Ct. 467, 38 L. Ed. 2d 427 (1973) – here, the defendant was searched after a lawful arrest, but argued that the discovery of narcotics violated the Fourth Amendment because law enforcement had exceeded the scope of a search authorized under the incident to arrest doctrine. The court, however, ruled that the search was not excessive as there is no requirement that officers only conduct a search for evidence of the crime for which the defendant was arrested.

[31] *Illinois v. Lafayette*, 462 U.S. 640, 103 S. Ct. 2605, 77 L. Ed. 2d 65 (1983) – defendant was arrested for disturbing the peace, and had his shoulder bag searched upon his arrival at the police station. The search of the shoulder bag revealed narcotics. The Supreme Court found that the Fourth Amendment was not violated because law enforcement officers maintained a right to search any containers found in the possession of a suspect when conducting inventory procedures after a valid arrest.

investigation of high technology crime should be cautious when attempting a search incident to an arrest involving a technological device. First, the court in *Tank* failed to consider that the purpose of the search incident to arrest doctrine was to provide officers with a means of ensuring the suspect had no weapons on their person and thereby provide protection for the arresting officer. It is unreasonable to believe that digital evidence can provide a physical threat to law enforcement officers.

The second problem with the *Tank* decision is the length of time between the seizure of the disk and the search of its contents. Numerous courts have held that lengthy searches after an arrest are invalid because over time the exigency of the situation disappears, therefore to avoid failing to meet this requirement it is required that the search be simultaneous with the arrest. There does, however, remain the question of what period of time after an arrest is considered acceptable? In *United States v. Reyes* (1996)[32], the court found that any evidence seized within the first twenty minutes of an arrest could be examined under the search incident to arrest doctrine. The search of a computer or a technological device will take far longer than twenty minutes because of the considerable storage capacities of the majority of technological devices in existence today. Of course, twenty minutes is enough time to complete a search of a floppy disk that only stores up to 1.4 MB of

---

[32] *United States v. Reyes*, 922 F. Supp. 818 (S.D. N.Y. 1996) – the defendant was arrested in connection to a narcotics investigation. Upon the defendant's arrest, a pager was obtained from the bag attached to his wheelchair. A second officer then searched the pager without a search warrant. It was the opinion of the court that no more than 20 minutes could have elapsed between the time of the arrest and the search of the pager, so the search was justified under the search incident to an arrest doctrine.

data, which is the equivalent of 500 pages of text or 25 to 30 image files. The search of a disk could not be authenticated by a desire to protect an officer from harm, and it is dangerous to conduct a warrantless search of a technological device without a search warrant, or without grounds for another warrantless search. For example, a warrantless seizure of a data disk or computer may be better justified under the exigent circumstance doctrine, in which the officer believes the data is in danger of being damaged or destroyed by the suspect and seizure is the only way to prevent the loss of the evidence. The actual search of the disk should be conducted under the authority of a valid search warrant.

Finally, the *Lafayette* decision, which was the basis of the *Tank* decision, was handed down at a time when there was little or no consideration of technology. When reading the court's decision, it appears it was their intent to provide a means of searching wallets, pocketbooks or briefcases to ensure that no weapons posing a threat to the officer were present. Today, many individuals do not carry pocketbooks and bulky briefcases, but instead carry a personal data assistant (PDA) that can store varying amounts of information. The warrantless search of a PDA found on a suspect after arrest is not encouraged as PDAs are not dangerous and they contain a large amount of data that cannot be searched within a short time. Law enforcement officers are encouraged to seize the technological device upon arrest of the individual in order to protect the data on the disk or device but to obtain a search warrant before they search the contents of the device.

Plain View Doctrine

The plain view doctrine can play a significant role in the investigation of crimes involving technology, if during the search of a computer for evidence of one form of criminal activity an investigator locates evidence of another form of criminal activity. A common example of this would be an officer who inadvertently discovers what he or she believes to be evidence of child pornography during a lawful search for evidence of narcotics trafficking. The question becomes can the officer open the files under the doctrine of plain view? If one follows the guidance of the tenth circuit in their decision for *United States v. Carey* (1999)[33], then the officer does have the right to seize such evidence under the plain view doctrine. The officer, however, must be involved in an active search for evidence and he or she must be in a place where they are legally allowed. The decision in *Carey* provided that law enforcement could not, however, begin a new search for additional evidence of the newly discovered criminal activity without additional justification from another warrantless search doctrine. If another warrantless search doctrine does not suitably address the issue, then a search warrant must be secured to continue searching for additional evidence of the criminal activity.

On the other side of this issue is the case of *United States v. Maxwell* (1996). In the *Maxwell* decision, the court of appeals for the armed forces found that a law enforcement officer violated the Fourth Amendment when he opened

---

[33] *United States v. Carey*, 172 F.3d 1268 (10th Cir. 1999) - Here the court ruled on plain view in regards to digital searches. Officers investigating evidence of an assault encountered evidence of an additional crime while searching a suspect's computer. The investigator then immediately abandoned his search for evidence of assault and began searching for evidence of the new crime. It was the opinion of the court that had the investigator stopped with the initial evidence then the evidence would have been admissible on an application for a search warrant.

files found under a different Internet screen name. The officer argued that the files from the additional screen name were admissible because they came into plain view during his search for child pornography, which was authorized by a search warrant. It was the opinion of the court that the files were not admissible under the plain view doctrine because the files had to be opened in order for them to be viewed. The court applied this doctrine in accordance with the case of *United States v. Villarreal* (1992)[34], in which the court found the plain view exception does not apply when officers have to open a closed container. The case of Maxwell is a military court decision, but it has been referenced in several cases concerning the plain view doctrine and as such bears careful consideration. As traditional crimes like murder, narcotics trafficking and stalking continue to involve the use of the Internet and computers; it is believed this will become a key legal argument.

Resseguie (1996) agrees with the court's decision in *Maxwell* and states his belief that investigators should never open a file that is outside of the search warrant's scope. This author, however, disagrees with Resseguie's reasoning and feels that with technology at its current level the *Carey* decision is currently the proper course of action

---

[34] *United States v. Villarreal*, 963 F.2d 770 (5th Cir. 1992) – U.S. Customs was alerted to the potential presence of narcotics in a 55-gallon drum. Upon the arrival of Customs agents, a search of the drum was conducted and marijuana was discovered. The officers then closed the drum and made a controlled delivery. Defendants appealed, arguing that their Fourth Amendment rights had been violated by the initial search. The court determined that an individual does maintain privacy in mailed items, but private carriers are allowed to search items mailed. In the case at hand, however, the search was conducted by government agents and was ruled unconstitutional.

to follow. Child pornography related files are usually video or picture files, and Resseguie argues that an officer looking for records of narcotics trafficking should be trained well enough to avoid opening a file that could be a picture or video file if their warrant does not specify pictures and videos. The problem is that the discovery of hidden files is not as easy as many may believe, and this leads to the argument that future court decisions could expand the powers granted law enforcement officers under the *Carey* decision.

Just such a scenario was encountered in the case of *United States v. Gray* (1999). In *Gray* the issue was whether a federal law enforcement officer had violated the Fourth Amendment when he opened images of child pornography while searching a computer storage device for records of another crime. The officer in question came across an image of child pornography during the course of a lawful search and argued that the images were admissible because they came into plain view during the course of his lawful search. The court agreed and admitted the images of child pornography, noting that the officer immediately stopped and obtained a new warrant for child pornography. Of interest was the court's conclusion that even if the officer had not obtained a new warrant, then the evidence would have still likely been admissible because the images would have come into plain view while the officer was in a place he had a lawful right to be.

Regardless of which approach law enforcement personnel choose to adhere to, it is recommended that extreme care be taken when opening files that are outside of their search warrant. The courts have found such an initial search to be acceptable with decisions such as the *Carey* decision; however, there is a strong likelihood that this issue may be challenged in the near future. To attempt opening any file under the plain view doctrine, it is required that law enforcement have gained access to the site via a search warrant, consent or another warrantless search exception. Further, upon the discovery of new evidence it is better to err on the side of caution and take the time to obtain a new search warrant.

Private Searches

The next warrantless search doctrine is that of searches by private citizens. When discussing the issue it should be noted the Supreme Court has ruled that the Fourth Amendment does not limit a private citizen when it comes to searches and seizures (*Walter v. United States*, 1980).[35] The issue of private searches was extended into searches of computers in the case of *United States v. Hall* (1998), where a computer repairman noticed several .jpeg files with names that led him to believe they could contain evidence of child pornography. This individual immediately notified his local law enforcement agency and the suspect was charged with possession of child pornography. Despite attempts by the defendant to argue to the contrary, the court refused to consider the computer repairman an agent of law enforcement, and as such found the repairman's actions were outside the protection of the Fourth Amendment.

---

[35] *Walter v. United States*, 447 U.S. 649, 100 S. Ct. 2395, 65 L. Ed. 2d 410 (1980) – defendant was arrested after a box containing videos of homosexual behavior was accidentally delivered to the wrong company. Law enforcement officers obtained the videos and viewed them without a search warrant. The defendant argued the search was illegal because the government had no right to view the films without a search warrant. It was the opinion of the court that the search was illegal, but did maintain that private citizens are not governed by the Fourth Amendment. In the case at hand, the court indicated they would have ruled differently had the private party first viewed the films before contacting law enforcement.

The court in *United States v. Barth* (1998) faced a similar situation, where the issue was whether an accountant's privacy was violated when a repairman searched his computer after inadvertently discovering images of child pornography during the course of a computer repair. Unlike the situation in the *Hall* case, the repairman in the *Barth* case notified law enforcement and then continued to search for additional images of child pornography without a search warrant. The court found the repairman's search illegal because he began working under color of state law from the moment he notified law enforcement about the first image of child pornography on the computer's hard drive.

In the *Barth* case, one of the factors the court mentioned was the fact the repairman worked occasionally as an informant. The court failed to place great emphasis on the issue, but it was mentioned when attempting to explain that the repairman should have known better than to continue searching for images of child pornography after the discovery of the original image. Investigators wishing to avoid having their evidence dismissed under a similar situation should ensure that individuals who alert them to the presence of digital evidence are aware of these decisions and their responsibilities.

There is recent evidence that the courts may be relaxing this approach. In one recent case the courts ruled that a hacker, who shut down child pornography websites and then contacted the FBI, was a private citizen. This ruling came despite the fact that the FBI had been in contact with this individual when they committed a similar act in the past. In fact, the FBI informed the hacker that they would not prosecute the hacker for possession of child pornography, so long as the materials were turned over to them after the conclusion of the investigation (Swaminatha, 2005).

This issue becomes even more critical when electronic communications are involved, a situation that many investigators encounter today. Under guidelines established by the Electronic Communications Privacy Act of 1986, an administrator of an Internet account may notify law enforcement if they encounter any communication they believe contains valuable evidence to a crime. Once the administrator contacts law enforcement then he or she will of course be considered an actor under color of state law and may no longer turn over evidence without proper legal authorization by a court order or search warrant. Investigators who work in communities where Internet service providers (ISP) operate should work to ensure that both law enforcement personnel and system administrators for the service provider are aware of the various courses of action that may be taken in such situations.

School Searches

The area of warrantless school searches is one area of jurisprudence that is in a massive state of transformation. The Supreme Court first encountered this issue in 1985 when they heard the case of *New Jersey v. T.L.O.* (1985)[36],

---

[36] *New Jersey v. T.L.O.*, 469 U.S. 325, 105 S. Ct. 733, 83 L. Ed. 2d 720 (1985) - In the case of *T.L.O.*, a teacher found two girls smoking cigarettes in the bathroom. The teacher took the girls to the office where the principal, upon learning the girls were smoking in the bathroom, emptied the girls' purses in a search for cigarettes. During the principal's search for cigarettes, he found rolling papers, which he knew was associated with the use of marijuana. He continued the search of the purse and found some marijuana, a pipe, a number of bills, and a list of people who appeared to owe T.L.O. money. The court ruled that school administrators have the right to search

where warrantless searches and seizures conducted on school grounds were found to be acceptable in certain situations. There are requirements and conditions to searches conducted under this doctrine, such as the individual school official must have reasonable belief that the student has violated either a law of the state or an infraction of the school's rules.

Several additional cases since *T.L.O.* have enhanced the understanding of warrantless searches on school grounds. Today, for example, it is generally accepted that a warrantless search may be based upon as little as reasonable suspicion. None of the cases has yet to involve direct mention of computers or technological devices, but opinions issued by the courts have laid a foundation for developments in the future. The *T.L.O.* decision itself established the belief that the need for an immediate response to situations that threaten the children, teachers, or educational process itself is what allows school administrators to conduct searches without a valid warrant.

The courts have held that the school official must contain a degree of certainty that behavior such as that discussed above is present before a warrantless search is acceptable. Of course, this level of certainty is rather small and in the case of *West Virginia v. Joseph T.* (1985), a school official was found to have legally searched and seized alcohol from a student's locker after another student reported that he had drank alcohol at another student's house the night before. The administrator claimed he was justified in searching the locker because there was reason to believe that the student would bring the alcohol to school and attempt to hide it after he had drank the night before.

---

belongings if they believe there is a threat to the school or a violation of school policies.

The ability to conduct a search without a warrant is easily granted in cases such as this, but the search must be kept within reason in regards to the crime believed to have been committed. If the search exceeds this acceptable level then the evidence will be removed from consideration (*Cales v. Howell*, 1985). In the *Cales* decision, it was determined that the strip search of a female student was unacceptable when the female was only cutting class and attempting to avoid a security guard.

So, what does this mean in terms of the possibility of computer searches? The search of a computer, or even a PDA, would require a belief that the device contained some form of information that is in violation of state or federal law, endangers the other students, or violates an established rule in the school system. The first of these possibilities to be considered is the issue of whether the computer, or PDA, is capable of violating state or federal law. Currently PDAs are not capable of extensive data manipulation, but the advent of portable keyboards may change this in the near future. Laptop computers could easily violate copyright laws but it would seem far-fetched to believe that school officials would consider a search of a computer for copyright violations. There is, however, the issue of networking. The ability of computers to network could lead to a situation where an individual could be using a laptop or PDA to transmit child pornography or engage in hacking activities prohibited under 18 U.S.C. 1030. In either situation, based upon the foundation laid down by the courts, the school administrator would appear to have the ability to search a computer or PDA for evidence of the crimes. The only consideration that might play in to the equation would be whether the search of a large storage medium is too intrusive. There have been no cases introduced to date that discuss whether this issue is one the courts would even consider.

Second, is the issue of whether the search of a laptop or PDA could be justified under the belief that fellow students are in danger? It is believed there are few situations in which school administrators would be able to justify the search and/or seizure of information or hardware from a laptop or PDA on this ground. Hacking and child pornography are crimes capable of harm to an individual, but it is hard to believe that an individual could use devices such as the ones discussed here in the production of child pornography on campus. Hacking, on the other hand, could be committed from the school grounds if the proper networking facilities were provided, but the hacks would rarely harm individuals in the school. Regardless, either of these two possible crimes would be more justified under the first issue discussed which involves violation of a law.

The third situation in which a warrantless search and seizure is justified on school grounds is when the activities of an individual violates an established school rule. Each of the above discussed issues, such as hacking and child pornography, would of course be sufficient to justify a warrantless search on the basis of violating a school's rules. Each of the aforementioned examples, however, would be superceded by the issue of the illegality of the acts. In considering this issue, the only situation that comes to mind would be the possibility that as more teachers become computer literate they may store their tests on computer disks. This could lead to situations where PDAs or laptops could contain information, such as the illegal copies of the tests that would violate the school rules and justify the search of the device. The school administrator, in a situation such as this, would have to possess a strong belief that the storage device contained copies of the illegal data.

Public versus Private Employer Searches

A subject that may be viewed in a similar fashion to that of school searches is the issue of search and seizure of computer-related evidence from a workplace computer. There are few cases that discuss the issue in regards to searches involving computers, but it is generally held that the Supreme Court decision of *O'Connor v. Ortega* (1987)[37] provides sufficient guidance on this issue (Kerr, 2001). There is no acceptance of a general rule regarding the search and seizure of government computers, but instead it has been generally held that every circumstance demands different consideration.

It is not impossible for an individual to maintain a reasonable expectation of privacy in a government work environment, but this expectation of privacy greatly diminishes when the individual's workspace is easily accessible by others in the office or by individuals who are allowed to enter the office space (Rhoden, 2002). Perhaps a good example of this would be a secretary who does not maintain a private office but only a desk on which their computer is located. If this desk is located in a general area through which many people are constantly moving past and around, then the secretary may have a hard time arguing that they have a reasonable expectation of privacy and that law enforcement entry to a computer without a search

---

[37] *O'Connor v. Ortega*, 480 U.S. 718 – here the court examined a search of a government physician's office and determined that an individual's expectation of privacy in the government workplace must be balanced with the employer's need to maintain control and order. A government search involving law enforcement officers does not in and of itself rule the search in violation of the Fourth Amendment as each case requires an individual assessment of whether a reasonable expectation of privacy exists.

warrant is in violation of the Fourth Amendment. It is worth noting that even a reasonable expectation of privacy does not bar a government employer from entering private workspace, if the intrusion is conducted as a means of investigating work-related activities or issues (*O'Conner v. Ortega*, 1987).

Searches involving private sector businesses normally invoke a greater expectation of privacy. According to Kerr (2001), a private sector search is equivalent to a search involving an individual's home and therefore requires a search warrant to search and seize a computer. There are, however, some situations where a search warrant is not required in a private sector work environment. If a co-worker or employer has common access to the computer, or perhaps even the area under consideration, then they may grant consent for law enforcement personnel to conduct a search. In considering both issues, private and public workplace searches, the expectation of privacy of an employee may be completely removed with well-drafted policies concerning the rights of employers to search computers and work areas at any time for any legitimate reason (Rhoden, 2002). These policies may range from documents dispersed at the time of hiring that indicates the employer's ability to conduct such searches, or the employer may elect to use a banner to inform their employees. A banner is merely a message that appears on the screen of a computer when turned on and the user logs into the system. This banner could inform users that their actions are subject to monitor by employers. Either method will greatly diminish the expectation of privacy an individual may maintain in their workplace.

Border Searches

The term border search refers to searches conducted at international border crossings and not to searches conducted at boundaries between states. Title 19 U.S.C. 482 states, "this provision gives Customs officers the authority to stop, search, and examine any vehicle, beast, or person entering the United States". This principle has withstood judicial scrutiny over the years. In the case of *Carroll v. United States* (1925), the Supreme Court found that law enforcement officers could not stop every vehicle on the highways on the chance of finding alcohol. This case is also important in the realm of border searches because the court did rule that a traveler might be stopped at an international border. It was the belief of the court that the need for national security and the protection of its citizens would supersede any considerations. This search would include any person or effects that come across the border including, but not limited to, luggage and international mail (*United States v. Scheer*, 1979). The court's rationale in the *Scheer* decision was the fact the individual is entering the country and the search is for the protection of United States citizens. As such, the need for security is great enough to enable a search even without the presence of probable cause. A border patrol or customs officer that encounters an individual at the border is allowed to search whatever and wherever he or she determines may contain illegal substances.

The case of *United States v. Ramsey* (1977) extended this issue, when the court was asked to determine whether or not an individual's personal mail could be opened without a warrant during a border search. Here, the court found the safety of citizens was so important that officials at the borders could search personal mail without a warrant or without even so much as probable cause. This is an important decision since the privacy rights an individual maintains in their personal mail should be as great as or greater than that of privacy in computers and laptops. Therefore, it stands to reason that the courts would more than likely rule the search and seizure of computers without a warrant to be valid.

Despite several searches, there appears to be few cases concerning the issue of computer technology and warrantless border searches. In the case of *United States v. Roberts* (2000), an individual was arrested as he attempted to leave the United States for Paris with child pornography in his possession. Law enforcement officers received information that Roberts was leaving the country and that he would possess child pornography on zip disks stored within his shaving kit. After Roberts' disks were seized, he admitted that he had child pornography on the disks but argued that they were for his own viewing pleasure and were not for sale. At his trial he moved to have the evidence dismissed because the officers had no right to stop him as he was leaving the country.

The Court determined that Roberts' claim had no merit and that Customs officials had a right to search any outgoing baggage by anyone entering or leaving the United States. Relying on prior cases in Fourth Amendment jurisprudence that stated computer storage mediums should be treated the same as a filing cabinet; the court determined that computers and storage disks could be searched at the border with or without a search warrant.

In another recent court decision, the issue was whether or not the Fourth Amendment applied to a search of a foreigner computer – a computer that was not located in the United States. Here, evidence was obtained from the computer via the Internet, and the argument was whether or not the Fourth Amendment applied to such a search. It was the opinion of the court that the issue of Fourth Amendment protections may be avoided if the computer being searched is not on domestic soil (Young, 2004). Of course there is still the consideration that the computer that conducted the search is on domestic soil. Therefore, if the evidence leaves an unprotected area but is received in a protected area, then does the Fourth Amendment apply? The answer to this question will be an interesting one that is sure to be addressed in the near future.

All aspects of warrantless cross border and border searches are sure to become increasingly scrutinized areas of Fourth Amendment debate in coming years. Several of the more dangerous high technology crimes involve individuals from other countries as perpetrators. For example, child pornographers and hackers from foreign countries are becoming more and more common. As investigations continue to go international, the rules concerning such activities must be clearly defined.

Previous discussions similar to this issue in regards to the protection of officers involved in the arrest process, such as automobile searches and searches incident to arrest, have dealt with the issue of time to search someone or their belongings. There does not appear to be any court rulings concerning the issue of time and border searches. In fact, a recent article circulated around the Internet by an unknown author discussed the use of computer disk scanning software that searches for various types of illegal software on the disks. The individual in question was unhappy when he discovered that customs officials in the United Kingdom were given the right to search through everyone's laptop computers. Currently, there is no documentation concerning the use of such software, but it is possible to design software that would scan for known catch phrases that are associated with child pornography, identity theft, hacking, and any other criminal activity. Regardless of whether or not the investigator decides to use a search warrant or whether he or she decides to attempt a warrantless search, it is important that the individual be aware of how the courts have interpreted the Fourth Amendment. Search and seizure is an extremely volatile area of case law, and the rapid rate of advances in technology will continue to force the courts to consider new facets of technology crime search and seizure. An investigator must be aware of his or her options at all times in order to justify their actions in the face of duty.

CHAPTER V

Recommendations for the Future

It has been shown that high technology crimes, whether considered computer crimes or cyber crimes, require law enforcement to adjust their investigative strategies. Since the development of computers and their introduction to students at MIT, computers and hacking have maintained a certain level of intrigue and interest for many individuals, some of which merely enjoy the opportunities the devices can provide to help them escape from their day-to-day lives. Others, however, feel that the computer is an important part of the future and they have a need to understand every aspect of operating the machinery. It is possible these individuals feel that to understand the technology that is to govern our society in the future is to maintain a certain level of control over the future.

Over the last few decades, the field of computer hacking has seen several changes, as well as what some would call milestones. Hackers like Kevin Mitnick, who is credited with being the first computer hacker to be featured on the FBI's most wanted list, have seen their computer-related lives go full circle. Mitnick has gone from the world's most feared dark side hacker to one of the world's most respected, and requested, computer security consultants. Others such as Kevin Poulsen have also traversed the boundaries between hacker, phreaker and law abiding computer user. Poulsen epitomized the ultimate fear when considering the crimes of phreaking and hacking because he began his foray into computer crime by engaging in phone phreaking "tricks" to impress himself and his friends. Over time, however, he began to engage in hacking with his computer. By using a combination of the two skills, Poulsen developed into one of the most dangerous hackers in history. Using his phone phreaking abilities, Poulsen was almost impossible to catch, and while his hacking never physically harmed anyone, there was always the potential for physical harm. Poulsen is also believed to have gained access to several matters of national security, a scenario that could result in physical harm for many individuals involved in the service of the federal government.

The contributions of Poulsen and Mitnick are still respected by many in the hacker subculture, but these individuals represent the past when discussing computer hacking. The current level of technology lends itself to the activities of those who do not wish to devote the time past hackers did to learn their trade. Poulsen and Mitnick both devoted a large percentage of their life to learning about computer programming and understanding how computers operated; skills that would assist them in their hacking endeavors. Many of today's hackers no longer believe they must devote large amounts of time to learning about computer programming, as free hacking utilities are available on numerous websites. In fact, these individuals have been termed script kiddies for their reliance on the script programs of others. Many believe these individuals are more dangerous than traditional hackers because they have very little understanding of what these free utility programs do to the networks they attack.

Hacking and phone phreaking are dangerous, but many consider these crimes to be more financially damaging than physically damaging. Child pornography and cyber stalking, two of the more frequently occurring crimes that have been termed to be cyber crimes, pose a significant physical and emotional danger to potential victims. Pornography involving children is used to convince kids that sexual activities with adults or other children are acceptable behaviors. If one also considers the emotional damage done to the child models of these images, it would be difficult to find another crime that is more damaging or physically threatening.

As the rate of computer related crimes continues to rise, there is the consideration of how to respond to these crimes. The field of criminal justice appears to be unprepared to handle these new crimes. Evidence of this is provided by the belief that as much as 75% of computer-related crime is not reported. Those responsible for this estimate concede that there are several reasons for such a low reporting rate, such as the fear some companies maintain that their clients would lose trust in their company if they discovered they were victimized (Economist, 2005), but it is also possible that there is a belief that law enforcement officers are not equipped to handle the investigation (Diliberto & Clark, 1996). If law enforcement agencies are to gain the trust of those they are charged to protect and to serve, these agencies must gain a better understanding of several legal and procedural issues that will impact their future investigations.

One potential answer to the problem lies in increased awareness provided by the academic community. Universities that offer programs in criminal justice, computer science, management information systems and other similar areas of study are placed in a unique situation when it comes to training individuals to investigate these crimes. If universities and academic departments were to take the initiative and begin offering more courses in this area then there is the chance that future law enforcement personnel and policy makers would have at a minimum a cursory understanding of the material and the problems facing society with the increased reliance on the computer as a criminal tool. Through teamwork and curriculum development a program in the investigation and prosecution of technology-assisted crimes could be developed.

There are several areas of procedure that require understanding, but this author has focused on the issue of search and seizure. Since the drafting of the Fourth Amendment, citizens of the United States have been protected against unreasonable searches of their persons, place or things. In discussing the term unreasonable, many legal scholars have argued that the best method of ensuring reasonableness is to draft an adequate search warrant. While this would appear at first glance to be a simple task, the preparation of a search warrant for digital evidence, or evidence of a computer related crime, is rather complex. In interpreting the Fourth Amendment in the physical realm, it has been held that a search warrant must be particular in regards to the items to be seized and specific in regards to where the search and seizure will take place. This doctrine becomes more complex when examining the issuance of a search warrant involving digital evidence.

The requirement of specificity is the lesser-debated side of search warrants involving evidence of a computer related crime. Generally, an investigator requesting a search warrant is able to provide the magistrate with specific information as to where the computer or other evidence is located. The requirement of particularity, however, is far more complex. Some scholars have argued that digital evidence could be located anywhere in the house and on one of several different forms of storage media. As such, when requesting a search warrant for digital evidence it has been suggested that investigators request a search warrant for "all digital media, including but not limited too...." At least one court, however, has struck down a search warrant including this statement, citing the warrant as overly broad.

On the other side of this issue is the ruling of another court, which has found that the inclusion of the statement does not void a search warrant. The problem with digital search warrants is the lack of direction provided by the United States Supreme Court. As of today, there are few rulings from the High Court concerning the issuance of search warrants for digital evidence. As such, the various circuit courts have been left to decide on the warrants. This has resulted in variation from circuit to circuit; a process that is even more confusing for circuits that may encounter this situation as an incident of first impression in the coming years. Investigators who handle investigations involving crimes committed with computers and technology must familiarize themselves with these various circuit decisions to prevent their evidence from being removed from trial.

Once the search warrant is secured then investigators must be careful and not damage the evidence as it is collected at the crime scene. To assist with this collection of evidence, some researchers have recommended the assembly of a computer search warrant team. This team would be comprised of various members who each specialize in a specific area of crime scene analysis. By using a collection of experts such as this, it is believed that investigators will avoid the more commonly encountered mistakes some law enforcement personnel make when handling computer related evidence. For example, by having someone skilled in the assembly of computers disassemble the computer and properly label the parts, the forensic investigator can easily reassemble the computer for examination.

For those agencies that cannot afford to assemble a team of specialists, there are several guides available from various federal law enforcement agencies. Both the United States Secret Service and the Department of Justice have prepared first responder guidelines. There are numerous problems, however, with both documents. Neither of the documents discusses the dangers of dealing with multiple operating systems. Both works merely assume that the suspect will be using the Microsoft Windows Operating System, an assumption that is somewhat reasonable as Windows is the number one operating system in use today. The problem is that execution of a search warrant following the guidelines for a Windows machine could potentially damage evidence should the agent encounter a Linux or Macintosh computer system.

Prior to this point, consideration has only been given to searches and seizures involving the use of a search warrant. Occasionally, however, there will develop a situation in which search or seizure involving digital evidence may be conducted without a search warrant. The Supreme Court has long recognized the need for warrantless searches in the physical world. The Supreme Court has ruled on few matters involving technology, but the circuit courts have ruled extensively on warrantless searches involving digital evidence. In examining warrantless search and seizure, the issue of privacy is one of the greatest considerations. A computer has recently been compared to an electronic filing cabinet. Other legal scholars have urged investigators to grant computers the same protections as that of not only a filing cabinet, but also a briefcase.

The various circuit courts have examined several of the warrantless search doctrines espoused by the Supreme Court and applied them to the search and seizure of digital evidence. In much the same manner as decisions regarding the issuance of an adequate search warrant, the Supreme Court has yet to rule on the various warrantless doctrines. A situation that has resulted in conflicting opinions between the various circuits in regards to warrantless searches. Perhaps the issue of plain view doctrine best represents an example of these problems. At least one lower court has ruled that law enforcement officers who are in the course of conducting a lawful search may open and view the first image of additional contraband discovered during a search of a computer or other technological storage device. On the other side of this issue, another court has ruled that evidence of separate criminal activity stored on a computer or technological device is not viewable under a search warrant for an entirely separate activity. As technology continuously improves, it will be interesting to see how the courts will handle issues like this in light of advancing technology.

In discussing the future impact of technology on the courts and their interpretations of the Fourth Amendment, it bears mentioning that new technology is not only affecting past judicial area, but is also leading the criminal justice system into new arenas. As technology and digital storage mediums have continued to improve in recent years, the courts have only recently begun to examine warrantless issues such as that of border searches involving digital storage devices. By using CD-ROMs and Zip disks a high tech criminal could potentially sneak in thousands of images or videos deemed illegal in the United States. This will lead the courts to further examine the issue of border searches, a warrantless search doctrine that was espoused as a means of preventing contraband from being allowed into or out of the United States. With advancements in technology, it is becoming increasingly important for individuals in the field of criminal justice to understand both how criminals are using computers and how the courts are interpreting traditionally physical realm opinions in light of technological advances. Many agencies can still argue that they have little or no need to handle high technology crime investigations, but the day is soon coming when all law enforcement personnel will face a high tech investigation. Understanding of how the courts are currently interpreting these search and seizure doctrines will place investigators in a far better situation when confronting technology crime cases as they reach their jurisdiction. It is the author's belief that few amendments are more difficult to understand than that of the Fourth Amendment, especially when considering the implications of technology in the interpretation. Personnel who wait until they are faced with a computer-assisted crime may find that it is too late to properly learn search and seizure techniques and may risk losing their evidence and ultimately their case.

Handling Digital Evidence

The need to abide by the Fourth Amendment is not one that is encouraged or recommended, it is required. Failure to properly follow the Fourth Amendment's guidance on search and seizure will result in the evidence from the seizure being removed from consideration. When examining the issue of search and seizure, the first consideration to make is in regards to satisfying the particularity requirement for a search warrant. With the discrepancies between the various circuit courts of appeals decisions, the question that arises is how should a search warrant be handled? A commonly used phrase included in search warrants is "including but not limited to..." Traditionally, this phrase was included on digital search warrants because of the need to ensure all forms of storage media were covered by the search warrant. Recently, however, some have begun to question whether the use of such wording generates a warrant that is "fishing" for evidence. Supporters of this statement argue that to list each item that could potentially contain digital evidence would place an undue burden on law enforcement. There are many different forms of digital storage available, but it hardly seems likely that the inclusion of all items would place an undue burden on law enforcement officials who investigate computer-related crimes. In fact, the inclusion of every item that could potentially contain evidence should be required on all search warrants, even warrants issued in circuits that have allowed the use of the phrase "including but not limited to...." This allows investigators to ensure that evidence is not seized only to later be removed from consideration. If during the search additional storage mediums are discovered, then a new search warrant may be obtained and the evidence protected until the warrant arrives.

The inclusion of every item that could potentially contain digital evidence has also been challenged because this generates a possible argument that the search is nothing more than a "fishing" expedition. Supporters of this argument believe that use of the limited phrasing allows investigators discretion at the time of the search, while the listing of all storage mediums creates a complete "fishing" expedition. Investigators who elect to list all potential storage mediums can provide protection from this criticism by merely ensuring that the magistrate issuing the warrant understands the importance, and the volatility, of digital evidence to the successful prosecution of the state's case. During the course of explaining this need, the investigator must ensure that the magistrate understands the need to examine all of the various storage mediums. Items seized that do not contain evidence of the crime for which the search warrant was issued will not be examined and will be released back to the owner. The magistrate must understand this as well, as it is this understanding that can prevent the "fishing" argument from being successfully employed.

Once the search warrant is obtained, there is the issue of executing the search warrant. A sample team outline has been provided for agencies that desire to develop a search warrant team to handle crime scenes involving computers and technological devices. The team outline consists of several members, but it is important to understand that not all agencies need to employ all new members. Many of the team members may be pulled from other law enforcement units within the agency. These individuals should receive adequate training concerning computers and digital evidence, but this does not mean that they should spend all of their time on the computer search warrant execution team. If an agency cannot afford to assemble this unit, then at a minimum several of their officers should undergo training to ensure they can handle a digital crime scene and respond in the same manner as that of a computer search warrant team.

Normally, the use of federal guidelines or training seminars would be recommended, but as previously shown there are several problems with the use of these guides. Agencies that will routinely handle investigations of computer-related crimes should either assemble their own set of guidelines similar to those recommended here, or should seek out a professional company that trains law enforcement personnel on the proper handling of a digital crime scene. Several of the bigger computer forensic companies provide training seminars relating to how to seize digital evidence and how to use their products to prepare a case.

The problems with the majority of the guidelines published involve their failure to cover the majority of situations that investigators will encounter during the execution of a search warrant for a computer-related crime. For example, the biggest problem this author has with the guidelines is their handling of shutting down the computer's operating system. The guidelines all agree that the solution to powering down a computer is to turn off the computer, and while this method is recommended for computers running Microsoft related operating systems, there are numerous dangers associated with conducting a hard shut-down of a computer running the Linux operating system. Powering down a Linux computer may result in the loss of valuable evidence. Granted, the majority of evidence that would be lost would relate to command line operations; however, this evidence may be important to a case involving a hacker. Command line operation is a term used to refer to commands that are ran from the command prompt, with the command prompt being closely related to the traditional DOS prompt screen. Here commands are ran by typing out the command. Linux is preferred by many hackers because of its command line use. With this in mind, a case involving a hacker may result in evidence being stored in the operating system's memory.

Because Linux updates its command line when the computer is shut down, powering down the computer without going through the power down process may result in loss of evidence. Additionally, some operating systems such as Linux and Macintosh may suffer from file integrity damage if they are not adequately shut down. With this in mind, it is recommended that an investigator always go through the proper shut down procedures when dealing with operating systems other than Microsoft systems. To clarify, the following must be considered: if an investigator fails to power down the computer running Linux then there is potential for lost evidence; likewise, if the investigator powers down the computer there is the potential for loss of evidence. Therefore, it seems apparent that if the potential for lost evidence is the same, the investigator should make every effort to ensure that the file system's integrity is not damaged. With operating systems such as Windows then of course it is recommended that the investigator powered down the computer by pulling the plug from the back of the computer.

If a computer criminal truly wants to protect his or her data from being seized then there are hundreds of methods of booby-trapping their computers. If an investigator attempts to counter all of the various methods, then it would require extensive training in order to execute a search warrant for digital evidence. Some professionals believe that computers can be booby-trapped with small explosives or with magnetic devices that will delete the data stored on the hard drive. While this is possible, it is also highly unlikely as the majority of computer related crimes investigated by law enforcement officials involves crimes such committed by less sophisticated criminals. This means that the majority of crimes investigated by law enforcement will deal with individuals who are not skilled enough to rig such devices. This is of course the most desirable scenario, but it is also the most unlikely due to financial considerations. Therefore, the use of this work, or any other guide, is preferable to an investigator not being

Recommendations for the Future

able to execute a search warrant because he or she has received absolutely no training.

Occasionally, an investigator will encounter a situation that calls for the search or seizure of digital evidence in the absence of a search warrant. Should such a scenario as this develop, it is of the utmost importance that the investigator has an understanding of how the courts have interpreted warrantless search doctrines in light of evolving technology. Failure to maintain this understanding could result in the invocation of the exclusionary rule, which means that the digital evidence will be removed from trial. Unlike more traditional crimes committed in the physical world, computer-related crimes leave little or no physical evidence. If an investigator damages or destroys digital evidence, then there is no case.

The biggest problem with understanding Fourth Amendment jurisprudence is the fact the Supreme Court has not ruled on many of the issues; a situation resulting in the issuance of conflicting decisions. In examining the various cases in recent years, some general guidelines can be pulled from the decisions. Generally, the courts have all agreed that a computer, storage medium or other technological storage device should be considered the equivalent of a filing cabinet. What this means is that searches conducted without a search warrant are not generally considered acceptable. The issue of privacy is an important consideration and one that drives the arguments behind most warrantless search doctrines.

In the previous chapter, eight warrantless search doctrines previously applied to searches for digital evidence was discussed. Based on the court cases discussed in this section, it is believed that few situations would allow for the search of a technological device. For example, the decision in *United States v. Tank* (9th Cir. 2000) might lead one to believe that a law enforcement officer can search a digital storage media immediately after an arrest. Despite the support this belief maintains in the legal community, the truth is that the circumstances in the Tank case are far from being such to extend a similar search to a computer-related device. The search incident to an arrest doctrine has long held that there is a two-pronged requirement for a valid warrantless search: first, there must be a legal arrest and second, the search must be contemporaneous with the lawful arrest. The searching of a pocket book may meet both prongs, but there is little doubt that searching storage media does not. It is unreasonable to believe that a law enforcement officer could search an entire CD-ROM, much less an entire laptop.

This does not mean, however, that a law enforcement officer does not maintain the right to seize a computer or other technological device under the search incident to arrest doctrine. In examining the exigent circumstances that allow for warrantless search and seizure, it becomes apparent there are several situations that would allow for the seizure of a computer or storage media. The exigent circumstances doctrine states that law enforcement officers are allowed to conduct a search and seizure when there is evidence that taking the time to obtain a search warrant could result in damage to the evidence or complete loss of the digital evidence. Cases like that of *United States v. David* (D. Nev. 1991) support this belief. An investigator who encounters a computer or storage device may elect to seize the computer under the exigent circumstances doctrine as long as the officer can articulate that a reasonable person would have also believed the evidence was in danger of being destroyed during the time required for a search warrant. Recent court decisions have even made seizures under this doctrine easier. According to the court in the *Illinois v. McArthur* (2001) opinion, a law enforcement officer has the right to prevent a suspect from gaining access to potential evidence while a search warrant is being requested. For this reason, it is the recommendation of this author that an investigator only use warrantless search doctrines to justify seizing a computer or other storage media. Once the device is seized and in custody, then a proper search warrant satisfying the requirements of particularity and specificity should be acquired.

The aforementioned statement does not apply to all warrantless search doctrines. Two doctrines would allow for warrantless searches of digital storage media. The first is in instances involving border searches. The Supreme Court has held that the safety needs of Americans are such that searches conducted at border entries do not require a search warrant. Instead, the investigator must be capable of justifying their desire to search a person or their belongings. With the events of September 11, 2001, still firmly in everyone's mind, this requirement may be at its lowest point ever. This does not make this form of search and seizure more appropriate. It does, however, explain why these searches may be allowed with greater frequency. The only problem with conducting searches and seizures at border points is the limited amount of impact these searches will play in the investigation of high technology crimes that will be investigated by state and local law enforcement agencies. Border searches are not going to solve most high tech crime investigations. Occasionally, an officer may uncover evidence of child pornography or identity theft during the course of one of these searches, but rarely will an investigation hinge on evidence uncovered from a warrantless border search.

The second warrantless exception that may provide benefit to investigators is that of the plain view exception. This exception has two areas of consideration. The first involves the discovery of digital storage media that could potentially contain evidence of a crime. For example, an officer executing a search warrant for evidence of business fraud may encounter a series of floppy disks that are labeled in such a manner that the officer believes the disks contain evidence of the crime. Once again, under this situation the officer may seize the disks and apply for a separate search warrant to examine the contents. The second version of the plain view exception deals with the examination of a computer or storage media. If an investigator is examining a computer for evidence of one crime and he or she inadvertently discovers evidence of another crime, then evidence of the new crime is admissible under the plain view doctrine. This evidence, however, does not grant an investigator the right to continue searching for additional evidence of this new crime. This newly discovered evidence is merely admissible in the application for an additional search warrant.

This second use of the plain view doctrine requires additional discussion. Many legal scholars have argued that there is no reason for an investigator to open a file with an extension outside the bounds of their search warrant. Traditionally, an investigator could identify these files by their file name extensions, such as .jpeg, .gif, .mpeg, or .avi. Today, this is not necessarily true. By merely changing the file name extension, a suspect can hide files. A .jpeg picture file can appear as a .doc document file with little or no prior technical experience. Deceptive techniques like this make an investigator's job significantly more difficult since every file on the computer must be examined in order to verify that the file is not a piece of evidence authorized under the search warrant. In searches involving this level of scrutiny, an investigator may encounter a different form of evidence during the course of a lawful and authorized search. Officers who are executing a search warrant are allowed to seize additional evidence of criminal activity as long as they are in a place they are allowed by law (*Arizona v. Hicks*, 1987). With this in mind, it is reasonable to believe that an officer who is executing a search warrant on a residence is allowed to enter various rooms during the course of his or her search. Should an officer encounter any evidence of criminal activity within a room of the residence, and the evidence is not moved to verify its illegality, then the evidence can be seized under the plain view doctrine. This author compares the opening of files on a computer to the searching of many rooms within a residence. Because files can be so easily hidden, it becomes necessary for an investigator to enter each room of a digital storage medium just as an officer would during the search of a physical residence. If an investigator encounters evidence of an additional crime then he or she should immediately end their search for evidence of the new crime and apply for an additional search warrant. To refuse the investigator the opportunity to search each file would be the equivalent of refusing an officer access to certain rooms within a residence. It is the hope of this author that future courts, when next facing this issue, will consider these facts and continue the line of reasoning developed in the decision of *United States v. Carey* (1999). Perhaps the courts will even build upon this decision and allow for the seizure of all evidence encountered during a lawful search.

Finally, there is the issue of consent in relation to searches involving digital evidence. Almost all courts have agreed that consent from an individual will void the need for a search warrant, but there are several dangers in using consent in place of a written search warrant. Perhaps the greatest danger lies in the ability of the owner of the property to withdraw their consent to the search. In the physical realm, it may take an investigator three or four minutes to search an address book based on consent. An electronic organizer, however, may take anywhere from five minutes to two hours. With such a great difference in time, there is a greater chance that the owner may change their mind and revoke the search. Even more dangerous is the fact that the individual may later claim they attempted to revoke their consent and they were denied the opportunity. It is for this reason that investigators who use consent as the basis for the search of a digital device should ensure they use an adequately drafted search warrant. The term adequately drafted is used to describe a document that provides the owner of the property with information relating to their right to withhold consent and what their consent will allow the investigator to search. Of course, not even the presence of a signed consent form removes the owner's right to revoke consent.

Just as in the issue of exigent circumstance and search incident to an arrest, an investigator who is attempting to search and seize a computerized device should use consent only as a means of seizing the device. The subsequent search of the contents should be conducted under the auspice of a properly drafted search warrant. This method may slow the process of the investigation down somewhat, but this slowness is assuredly preferable to having the evidence removed completely from trial.

As evidenced by the court cases and previous discussions, the issue of search and seizure does not always contain a clear-cut line in which an investigator can make a determination of whether to seize digital evidence with or without a warrant. There is, however, one general concession among the courts, and that is the belief that a search warrant prevents a search from being considered excessive or unreasonable. Therefore, it is important that investigators in the field of criminal justice understand that there are situations that would allow for a search or seizure without a warrant, but these circumstances are wrought with danger. It is better for an investigator to take the extra time to draft a search warrant before conducting a search of a digital device.

Of course, this recommendation does not stand for every case. As already stated, there are no clearly defined lines in the realm of search and seizure. Following the recommendations provided here will, however, allow an investigator the best possible opportunity for ensuring the proper collection of digital evidence. After all, if the remaining option is the possibility of losing the evidence, then it stands to reason that taking extra care during the search will only benefit the parties involved. All investigators need to gain this level of understanding in regards to search and seizure of technological devices and digital storage media, as the future is sure to hold an increase in reliance on this form of technology for the commission of crimes.

Law enforcement personnel who do not take the necessary time today will find themselves racing to catch up in the future, and this is a race in which law enforcement agencies are likely to lose, as the criminal element is already preparing and has the head start. The solution is to begin keeping pace with those who would misuse technology while there is still time. Failure to follow this advice will only worsen the ability of law enforcement to investigate crimes involving technology; a situation that will in turn only lessen the faith of those law enforcement are dedicated to protect and to serve. This is a scenario that individuals in the criminal justice field cannot allow to unfold. Responses must be developed now and implemented soon; otherwise, there is little hope for successful combating of the high technology crime problem.

REFERENCES

Akdeniz, Y. (1999). *Sex on the net: the dilemma of policing cyberspace.* United Kingdom: Garnett Publishing.

Avenger. (1991). Beginning to advanced carding. Retrieved March 28, 2002 from http://www.textfiles.com/anarch/CARDING/.

Bare bones of child pornography. (2002). Retrieved April 15, 2002 from http://wwww.safe4kids.org/reports/cporn2.htm.

Baron-Evans, A. (2003). When the government seizes and searches your client's computer. *Champion.* 27-JUN Champion 18-25.

Baron-Evans, A. & Murphy, M. (2003). The fourth amendment in the digital age: some basics on computer searches. *Boston Bar Journal.* 47 B.B.J. 10-13.

Berg, T. (2004). Practical issues in searching and seizing computers. *Thomas M. Cooley Journal of Practical and Clinical Law.* 7 T.M. Cooley J. Prac. & Clinical L. 27-50.

Bernstein, N. (1997). Inmate accused of collecting child pornography. (1997, March 28) *New York Times*, p. A16.

Bequai, August. (1978). *Computer crime.* Massachusetts: Lexington Books.

Bequai, August. (1987). *Technocrimes.* Massachusetts: Lexington Books.

Blue Ridge Thunder Website (2001). Retrieved August 21, 2001, from http://www.blueridgethunder.com.

Bohn, R. & Muster, L. (2003). The dawn of the computer age: how the fourth amendment applies to warrant searches and seizures of electronically stored information. *Suffolk Journal of Trial & Appellate Advocacy.* 8 Suffolk J. Trial & App. Adv. 63-80.

Bonisteel, S. (2002). Identity theft insurance going mainstream. *News Bytes News Network.* Retrieved April 28, 2002, from EBSCOHost database.

Book, C. (2004). Do you really know who is on the other side of your computer screen? stopping internet crimes against children. *Albany Law Journal of Science & Technology.* 14 Alb. L.J. Sci. & Tech. 749-774.

Brail, S. (1996). The price of admission: harassment and free speech in the wild, wild west. In L. Cherny and E. Wise (Eds.) *Wired women: gender and new realities in cyberspace.* Washington: Seal Press.

Brenner, S. (2001). Defining cybercrime: a review of state and federal law. In R. D. Clifford (Ed.) *Cybercrime: the investigation, prosecution and defense of a computer-related crime* (pp. 11-69). Durham, N.C.: Carolina Academic Press.

Brenner, S. (2004). Cybercrime metrics: old wine, new bottles? *Virginia Journal of Law & Technology.* 9 Va. J.L. & Tech. 13-111.

Brenner, S. & Frederiksen, B. (2002). Computer searches and seizures: some unresolved issues. *Michigan Telecommunications and Technology Law Review.* 8 Mich. Telecomm. & Tech. L. Rev. 39-114.

Brenner, S. & Koops, B. (2004). Approaches to cybercrime jurisdiction. *Journal of High Technology Law.* 4 J. High Tech. L. 1-46.

Buford, T. (2002). Your child and pornography. Madison, TN: Tommera Press. Electronic version available: http://www.firesofdarkness.com.

Burstow, P. (2002). Pedophilia and the internet. Retrieved April 15, 2002 from http://www.zyworld.com/paul burstow/paedoarticle.htm.

Campbell, D. (2002). LAPD slow to help in identity theft. *Los Angeles Times*. Retrieved April 28, 2002, from EBSCOHost database.

Carter, A. & Perry, A. (2004). Computer crimes. *The American Criminal Law Review*. 41 Am. Crim. L. Rev. 313-365.

Casanova, M. (2000). The history of child pornography on the internet. *Journal of Sex Education and Therapy*, 25, 245-252.

Casey, E. (2000). *Digital evidence and computer crime: forensic science, computers and the internet.* New York: Academic Press.

Child molesters and the internet. (2002). Retrieved April 15, 2002 from http://www.kidsap.org/ChildMolesters AndTheIntenet.htm.

Clark, F. & Diliberto, K. (1996). *Investigating computer crime.* New York: CRC Press.

Computer Fraud and Abuse Act. 18 U.S.C. 1030 (1989); Amended 1996, 2001.

Coutorie, L. (1995). The future of high-technology crime: a parallel Delphi study. *Journal of Criminal Justice*, 23, 13-28.

Dearne, K. (2001). Cyber crime costs are increasing. *The Australian*. Edition 1, pg. 36. Retrieved August 21, 2001, from EBSCOHost database.

Denning, P. (1990). *Computers under attack: intruders, worms, and viruses.* New York: ACM Press.

Diffie, W. and Landau, S. (1998). *Privacy on the line: the politics of wiretapping and encryption.* Massachusetts: The MIT Press.

Dillon, S., Groene, D. & Hayward, T. (1998). Computer crimes. *American Criminal Law Review* 35, 503-547.

D.K. (1996). Hacker history. *America's Network.* 100(14), 42-43.

Doege, D. (2002). Milwaukee-area officials say identity theft is lucrative, rapidly growing. *The Milwaukee Journal Sentinel.* Retrieved April 28, 2002, from EBSCOHost database.

Donohue, L. & Walsh, J. (2001). Patriot act – a remedy for an unidentified problem. *San Francisco Chronicle.* October 30, 2002.

Draper, J. (2001). How cap'n crunch became a phone phreaker. Retrieved May 25, 2002 from http://www.techtv.com/screensavers/supergeek/story/0, 24330,334781,00.html.

Author Unknown (2005). Forensic computer: as criminals and crime-fighters go digital, analyzing clues from computers is a growing field. *Economist,* 374(8417), Retrieved on May 12, 2005, from the EBSOHost Database.

Edgett, S. (2003). Double-clicking on fourth amendment protection: encryption creates a reasonable expectation of privacy. *Pepperdine Law Review.* 30 Pepp. L. Rev. 339-366.

Electronics Communication Privacy Act. 18 U.S.C. 2510-2522 (1986); Amended 2001.

Electronic Freedom Foundation. (2002). Privacy, surveillance and terrorism. Retrieved October 12, 2002, from http://www.eff.org.

Elliot, C. (2002). Identity theft becoming more common, government warns. *South Bend Tribune.* Retrieved April 28, 2002, from EBSCOHost database.

Estrella, A. (2001). The lowdown on e-mail, surfing the Internet at work. Retrieved November 15, 2000

http://pacific.bizjournals.com/pacific/stories/2001/08/27/focus4.html.
Florida Department of Law Enforcement (FDLE) (2002). LEACH task force agents arrest a south florida "traveler". Retrieved December 7, 2002, from http://www.flde.state.fl.us/press_releases/20020405_andrew_hochstadt.html.
Flowers, R. (1996). *The victimization and exploitation of women and children: a study of physical, mental, and sexual maltreatment in the United States.* Jefferson, North Carolina: McFarland & Company.
Freedom of Information Act. 5 U.S.C. s/s 552 (1966); Amended 1996.
Freeh, L. (2002). A parent's guide to internet safety. U.S. Department of Justice Federal Bureau of Investigation Publications. Retrieved April 15, 2002 from http://www.fbi.gov/publications/pguide/pguidee.htm.
Fuentes, A. (1996). Who opened their e-mail? *Village Voice*, 41, 15.
Gill, J. (2001). One of the world's most feared hackers switches sides. *Sunday Business.* Retrieved March 25, 2002, from EBSCOHost database.
Gindin, S. (1999). Guide to e-mail and the internet in the workplace. *Bureau of National Affairs, Inc.* Retrieved December 8, 2002, from http://www.info-law.com/guide.html.
Goldstein, A. (2002). Credit-card firms look to stop fraud with new authentication technologies. *The Dallas Morning News.* Retrieved April 28, 2002, from EBSCOHost database.
Guidance Software. (2002). Encase. Retrieved October 5, 2002, from http://www.guidancesoftware.com.

Hafner, K. & Markoff, J. (1991). *Cyberpunk: outlaws and hackers on the computer frontier.* New York: Simon & Schuster.

Hallifax, J. (2001). Inmate accused identity theft ring. *Associated Press Online.* Retrieved April 28, 2002, from EBSCOHost database.

Hermann, M. (1998) *Search and seizure checklists.* St. Paul, Minnesota: West Group.

Hopper, D. (2002). Reports on identity theft on rise. *Associated Press Online.* Retrieved April 28, 2002, from EBSCOHost database.

Howard, T. (2004). Don't cache out your case: prosecuting child pornography possession laws based on images located in temporary internet files. *Berkeley Technology Law Journal.* 19 Berkeley Tech. L.J. 1227-1273.

Jacobsen, H. and Green R. (2002). Computer crimes. *American Criminal Law Review* 39, 273-325.

Jenkins, P. (2001). *Beyond tolerance: child pornography online.* New York: University Press.

Kaplan, D. (1997). New cybercop tricks to fight child porn. *U.S. News and World Report*, 122, 29.

Kerr, O. (2001). Searching and seizing computers and obtaining electronic evidence in criminal investigations. *Computer Crime and Intellectual Property Section (CCIPS).* Retrieved on April 15, 2002, from: http://www.cybercrime.gov/searchmanual.htm.

Kerr, O. (2005). Digital evidence and the new criminal procedure. *Columbia Law Review.* 105 Colum. L. Rev. 279-318.

Kitchen hand clicks his way to cyber-fraud history. (2001). *The Australian.* Retrieved April 28, 2002, from EBSCOHost database.

Ko, J. (2004). The fourth amendment and the wiretap act fail to protect against random ISP monitoring of e-mails for the purpose of assisting law enforcement. *The John Marshall Journal of Computer & Information Law.* 22 J. Marshall J. Computer & Info. L. 493-533.

Ko, M. (2002). Porn-busters, beware. Retrieved December 8, 2002, from http://www.marnieko.com/pornbusters.htm.

Kornblum, Janet. (1997). Mitnick faces 22-month rap. Retrieved July 20, 2001, from http://www.cnetnews.com.

Krane, J. (2002). Cops chase drugs on the internet. March 20, 2002 from www.entheogen.com.

Kreston, S. (2004). Computer search and seizure issues in internet crimes against children cases. *Rutgers Computer and Technology Law Journal.* 30 Rutgers Computer & Tech. L.J. 327-373.

Kruse, W. and Heiser, J. (2002). *Computer forensics: incident response essentials.* New York: Addison-Wesley Pub.

Levy, S. (1994). *Hackers: heroes of the computer revolution.* New York: Penguin Books.

Littman, J. (1996). *The fugitive game: online with Kevin Mitnick.* Boston: Little Brown and Company.

Littman, J. (1997). *The watchman: the twisted life and crimes of serial hacker Kevin Poulsen.* Boston: Little Brown and Company.

Lohse, D. (2001). IRS error causes san Francisco-area taxpayers receive others' documents. *San Jose Mercury News.* Retrieved April 28, 2002, from EBSCOHost database.

Mandia, K. and Prosise, C. (2001). *Incident response: investigating computer crime.* San Francisco: McGraw-Hill Osborne Media.

McCabe, K. (2000). Child pornography and the internet. *Social Science Computer Review*, 18, 73-76.

McChrystal, M., Gleisner, W., & Kuborn, M. (1998). Law enforcement in cyberspace: search and seizure of computer data. *Wisconsin Lawyer*. 71-DEC Wis. Law. 35-37.

McGraw, D. (1995). Sexual harassment in cyberspace: the problem of unwelcome e-mail. *Rutgers Computer and Technology Law Journal*, 21, 491-518.

Meinel, C. (2000). *Uberhacker! How to break into computers*. Washington: Loompanics.

Mercer, L. (2004). Computer forensics characteristics and preservation of digital evidence. *FBI Law Enforcement Bulletin*. 73(3), 28-32.

Moad, J. (2001). Tracking down the nasty guys. *EWeek*, 18, 40-41.

National Institute of Justice. (2001). Electronic crime scene investigation: a guide for first responders. Retrieved on August 15, 2002, from http://www.ojp.usdoj.gov/nij.

National White Collar Crime Center. (2002). Identity theft. Retrieved August 15, 2002, from http://nw3c.com.

Nesteroff, G. (1997). Phreak show. Retrieved December 5, 2002 from http://www.peak.sfu.ca/the-peak/97-1/issue3/phreak.html.

Newman, J. (1999). *Identity theft: the cybercrime of the new millennium*. Port Townsend, Washington: Loompanics.

Paradise, P. R. (1999). *Trademark counterfeiting, product piracy, and the billion dollar threat to the U.S. economy*. Connecticut: Quorum Books.

Parker, D. (1976). *Crime by computer*. New York: Scribner.

References

Patzakis, J. (2002). The encase process. *Handbook of computer crime investigations: forensic tools and technology.* San Francisco: Academic Press. Pp. 53-72.

Penenberg, Adam L. (1999). The demonizing of a hacker. *Forbes* Retrieved June 12, 2001 from http://www.forbes.com.

Platt, C. (1996). *Anarchy online: net sex. the truth behind the hype.* New York: HarperPrism.

Power, R. (2000). *Tangled web: tales of digital crime from the shadows of cyberspace.* Indianapolis, Indiana: Que.

Radcliff, D. (2000). Vigilante group targets child pornography sites. *Computerworld,* 34, 40.

Resseguie, D. (2000). Computer searches and seizures. *Cleveland State Law Review,* 185-214.

Rhoden, C. (2002). Challenging searches and seizures of computers at home or in the office: from a reasonable expectation of privacy to fruit of the poisonous tree and beyond. *American Journal of Criminal Law. 30 Am. J. Crim. L. 107-134.*

Royal Canadian Mounted Police. (2001) RCMP. Retrieved on March 22, 2002, from http://www.rcmp-grc.cg.ca/html/cpu-cri.htm.

Sanders, E. (2001). Children's online file swapping often yields porn, report says. (2001, July 28). *Los Angeles Times.*

Section of U.S. Code covering the rights of Customs agents in regards to border searches. Title 19 U.S.C. 482.

Seeger, S. & Visconte, V. (1997). Fourth amendment ramifications of cyberspace surveillance. Retrieved on February 25, 2001 from http://wings.buffalo.edu/law/complaw.

Seward, J. & Austin, D. (2004). E-sleuthing and the art of electronic data retrieval: uncovering hidden assets in the digital age. *American Bankruptcy Institute Journal.* 23-FEB AMBKRIJ 14-51.

Sigal, P. (2002). AOL suit highlights danger of internet theft. *The Philadelphia Inquirer.* Retrieved April 28, 2002, from EBSCOHost database.

Simon, D. & Jones, R. (2004). Intellectual property crimes in the cyber world. *Wisconsin Lawyer.* 77-OCT Wis. Law. 12-17.

Stamberg, S. (2001). Analysis: sale of state birth and death records temporarily suspended in california. *Morning Edition (NPR).* Retrieved April 28, 2002, from EBSCOHost database.

Statistical Analysis Center. (2002). Information and technology capabilities of Mississippi law enforcement agencies. Retrieved on December 8, 2002, from http://www.usm.edu/mssac/publications/ms_sac_public ations.htm.

Still, J. (2003). Grooming causes significant harm. *Community Care*, 1461, 21.

Suspected love bug creator to give up hacking: report. Retrieved June 15, 2001 from http://www.antionline. com.

Swaminatha, T. (2005). The fourth amendment unplugged: electronic evidence issues & wireless defenses. *Yale Journal of Law and Technology.* 7 Yale J.L. & Tech. 51-65.

This eldrick woods...what's he look like? (2000). *Los Angeles Times.* Retrieved April 28, 2002, from EBSCOHost database.

Tran, M. (2001). New law forces police to do an about-face on identity theft. *Los Angeles Times.* Retrieved April 28, 2002, from EBSCOHost database.

Trigaux, Robert. (2000). A history of hacking. *St. Petersburg Times* Retrieved June 15, 2001 from http://www.sptimes.com/Hackers/history.hacking.html.

United States House of Representatives. (2001). Children's access to pornography through internet file-sharing programs. Retrieved on August 15, 2002, from www.house.gov/reform/min/pdfs/ pdf_inves/pdf_pornog_rep.pdf.

Uniting and Strengthening America by Providing Appropriate Tools Required to Intercept and Obstruct Terrorism Act. H.R. 3162 (October 24, 2001).

Verton, D. (2001). Identity thefts skyrocket, but less than 1% occur online. *Computerworld*, 35, 7-11.

Wall, C. & Paroff, J. (2004). Cracking the computer forensics mystery. *Utah Bar Journal.* 17-OCT Utah B.J. 10-15.

Wang, W. (1998). *Steal this computer book: what they won't tell you about the internet.* San Francisco: No Starch Press.

Wang, W. (2001). *Steal this computer book 2: what they won't tell you about the internet.* San Francisco: No Starch Press.

Wayner, P. (2002). *Disappearing cryptography – information hiding: steganography and watermarking.* San Francisco: Morgan Kaufmann Publishers.

Weber, G. (2002). Grooming children for sexual molestation. Retrieved April 15, 2002 from http://www.vachss.com/guest_dispatches/grooming.html.

Wilson, D. (2001). Life is not a movie, and other hacker truths. (2001, August 19). *Los Angeles Times.*

Wolf, J. (2001). Grooming: the process of victimization. Retrieved on May 24, 2002 from http://www.cachouston.org/pressroom/library/feature%20articles/grooming.pdf.

Wright, O. (2001). Identity theft drives wrong man into court. *The Times*. Retrieved April 28, 2002, from EBSCOHost database.

Young, S. (2004). Verdugo in cyberspace: boundaries of fourth amendment rights for foreign nationals in cybercrime cases. *Michigan Telecommunications and Technology Law Review*. 10 Mich. Telecomm. & Tech. L. Rev. 139-174.

Zaenglein, N. (2000). *Secret software*. Boulder, CO: Paladin Press.

Zipp, J. (2005). Fourth amendment limitations on the execution of computer searches conducted pursuant to a warrant. *Columbia Law Review*. 105 Colum. L. Rev. 841-872.

Court Decisions

Ashcroft v. Free Speech Coalition, 535 U.S. 234, 122 S. Ct. 1389, 152 L. Ed. 2d 403 (2002).

Alana Shoars v. Epson America Inc., No. B 073234 (1994).

Arizona v. Hicks, 480 U.S. 321, 107 S. Ct. 1149, 94 L. Ed. 2d 347 (1987).

Boyd v. United States, 116 U.S. 616, 6 S. Ct. 524, 29 L. Ed. 746 (1886).

Bumper v. North Carolina, 391 U.S. 543, 88 S. Ct. 1788, 20 L. Ed. 2d 797 (1968).

Cales v. Howell, 635 F.Supp. 454 (E.D. Mich. 1985).

Carroll v. United States, 267 U.S. 132, 45 S. Ct. 280, 69 L. Ed. 543 (1925).

Chimel v. California, 395 U.S. 752, 89 S. Ct. 2034, 23 L. Ed. 2d 685 (1969).

References

Daubert v. Merrell Dow Pharmaceuticals, 509 U.S. 579, 113 S. Ct. 2786, 125 L. Ed. 2d 469 (1993).
Davis v. State, 497 So. 2d 1344 (Fla. 5d 1986).
Frye v. United States, 293 F. 1013 (D.C. Cir. 1923).
Illinois v. Lafayette, 463 U.S. 640, 103 S. Ct. 2605, 77 L. Ed. 2d 65 (1983).
Illinois v. McArthur, 531 U.S. 326, 121 S. Ct. 946, 148 L. Ed. 2d 838 (2001).
Illinois v. Rodriguez, 497 U.S. 177, 110 S. Ct. 2793, 111 L. Ed. 2d 148 (1990).
Johnson v. United States, 333 U.S. 10, 68 S. Ct. 367, 92 L. Ed. 436 (1948).
Jimenez v. State, 643 So. 2d 70 (Fla. 2d DCA 1994).
Matter of Search Warrant for K-Sports Imports Inc., 163 F.R.D. 594 (C.D. Cal. 1995).
New Jersey v. T.L.O., 469 U.S. 325, 105 S. Ct. 733, 83 L. Ed. 2d 720 (1985).
Ohio v. Robinette, 519 U.S. 33, 117 S. Ct. 417, 136 L. Ed. 2d 347 (1996).
O'Connor v. Ortega, 480 U.S. 709; 107 S. Ct. 1492; 94 L. Ed. 2d 714
Parkhurst v. Trapp, 77 F.3d 707 (3rd Cir. 1996).
Preston v. United States, 376 U.S. 364, 84 S. Ct. 881, 11 L. Ed. 2d 777 (1964).
Schneckloth v. Bustamonte, 412 U.S. 218, 93 S. Ct. 2041, 36 L. Ed. 2d 854 (1973).
State v. Hammonds, 557 So. 2d 179 (Fla. 3d DCA 1990).
Stoner v. California, 376 U.S. 483, 84 S. Ct. 889, 11 L. Ed. 2d 856 (1964).
United States v. Alfonso, 759 F.2d 728 (9th cir. 1985).
United States v. Ball, 90 F.3d 260 (8th Cir. 1996).
United States v. Barth, 26 F.Supp.2d 929 (1998).
United States v. Bizier, 111 F.3d 214 (1st Cir. 1997).
United States v. Blas, No. 90-Cr-162 (E.D. Wis. 1990).

United States v. Bradshaw, 102 F.3d 204 (6th Cir. 1996).
United States v. Burns, 37 F.3d 276 (7th Cir. 1994).
United States v. Carey, 172 F.3d 1268 (10th Cir. 1999).
United States v. Charbonneau, 979 F. Supp. 1177 (S.D, Ohio 1997).
United States v. David, 756 F. Supp. 1385 (D. Nev. 1991).
United States v. Durham, 1998 WL 684241 (D. Kan. 1998).
United States v. Elliot, 50 F.3d 180 (2d Cir. 1995).
United States v. Gray, 78 F. Supp. 2d 5244 (E.D. Va. 1999).
United States v. Haddad, 558 F.2d 968 (9th Cir. 1977).
United States v. Hall, 142 F.3d 988 (7th Cir. 1998).
United States v. Hambrick, 55 F. Supp.2d 504 (W.D. Va. 1999).
United States v. Hunter, 13 F. Supp. 2d 574 (D. Vt. 1998).
United States v. Lyons, 992 F. 2d 1029 (10th Cir. 1993).
United States v. Matlock, 415 U.S. 164, 94 S. Ct. 988, 39 L. Ed. 2d 242 (1974).
United States v. Maxwell, 45 M.J. 406 (C.A.A.F. 1996).
United States v. Moorehead, 57 F.3d 875 (1995).
United States v. Ortiz, 84 F.3d 977 (7th Cir. 1996).
United States v. Poulsen, 41 F.3d 1330 (9th Cir. 1994).
United States v. Rahme, 813 F.2d 31 (2nd Cir. 1987).
United States v. Ramsey, 431 U.S. 606 (1977).
United States v. Reed, 15 F.3d 928 (9th Cir. 1994).
United States v. Reyes, 922 F. Supp. 818 (S.D.N.Y. 1996).
United States v. Robinson, 414 U.S. 218, 94 S. Ct. 467, 38 L. Ed. 2d 427 (1973).
United States v. Roberts, 86 F. Supp. 2d 678 (S.D. Texas 2000).
United States v. Romero-Garcia, 991 F. Supp. 1223 (D. Or. 1997).
United States v. Ross, 456 U.S. 798 (1982).
United States v. Scheer, 600 F.2d 5 (3d Cir. 1979).

United States v. Smith, 27 F. Supp. 2d 1111 (C.D.Ill. 1998)
United States v. Tank, 200 F.3d 627 (9th Cir. 2000).
United States v. Tucker, 150 F.Supp.2d 1263 (D. Utah 2001).
United States v. Upham, 168 F.3d 532 (1st Cir. 1999).
United States v. Villarreal, 963 F.2d 770 (5th Cir. 1992).
Walter v. United States, 447 U.S. 649 (1980).
Warden v. Hayden, 387 U.S. 294, 87 S. Ct. 1642, 18 L. Ed. 2d 782 (1967).
West Virginia v. Joseph T., 336 S.E.2d 728 (W. Va. 1985).

APPENDIX A

Relevant Terminology

For many individuals the world of high technology crime and computer concepts can be confusing and sometimes frustrating because of the vast amount of new terminology, phrases, and acronyms. In an attempt to alleviate such confusion the following section will consist of a listing of important terminology relating to the subject matter. It should be noted that this list is by no means exhaustive, as there are entire dictionaries written on computer technology related terms.

ARPANET – Advanced Research Projects Agency Network – This is the precursor to the Internet, established in 1969, this was the first time four computers from different areas of the United States were linked together.

Anonymous Remailer – This is an e-mail service allowing users to send e-mails without identifying who they are or from what computer they originated.

ATA – Anti Terrorist Act – This was the title of the original terrorist reform acts discussed after September 11, 2001. This legislation was highly debated because 1) it made computer crimes such as hacking a crime punishable by life in prison without parole and 2) it gave law enforcement broad investigative powers and set no time line in which these powers would expire.

BIOS – Basic Input Output System – This system controls how data is handled by the computer. Every program that runs on a computer communicates with the BIOS in order to operate.

Bit Copy – This is the term used to describe an exact disk image that computer forensic software can create. Traditional copies only copy the files that are currently active on the hard drive. A bit copy will copy every character that is saved on a hard drive; many times the hidden space will contain valuable evidence.

Brute Force Attack – This is when a hacker will attempt to guess a login and password to gain access to a computer system. The hacker may do the guessing manually or they may run a brute force dictionary attack, where a program will go through the dictionary trying all combinations of words.

Bulletin Board Service – This is also known as a BBS, and is computers that are administered by individuals and allow the users to dial in using their modem and chat with other users, download files, or send e-mails.

Byte – This is the lowest used form of storage for digital media.

Child Pornography – This is any video or image that depicts a child under the age of 18 years old engaged in a sexual pose or act. The image or video can be a physical copy or a digital copy. Due to the recent decision of *Ashcroft v. Free Speech Coalition*, 535 U.S. 234 (2002), law enforcement must be able to prove that the child in the picture or video is under the age of 18 years.

Clusters – These are collections of bits (characters) on a hard disk. The number of bits per cluster is determined by which file allocation table is being used. If 16kb of data per cluster is used and there is a document file 20k in size, then the file will take up one entire cluster and 4kb of another cluster. The remaining space cannot be used by another file and becomes dead space, also known as slack space.

Computer Crime – This is any crime that involves the use of a computer in its commission and is enumerated in the statutes. The computer itself can be an instrument of the crime or it may be the fruit of the crime. The most common statute used to prosecute these crimes is 18 U.S.C. 1029 (Computer Fraud and Abuse Act of 1989).

Cracker – This is someone who cracks passwords or cracks software protection in order to make illegal copies. True hackers claim that this is the term that should be used to describe individuals who break into computers, because they are not true hackers but are instead criminal hackers, henceforth the term cracker.

Credit Card Skimming – This refers to the practice of stealing credit card numbers and owner information using a small device that captures all of the information when the card is ran through the reader, known as a skimmer.

Crimoid – This is an elegant or media enhanced computer attack. The term was coined by Denning to describe his and Van Duyn's listing of computer attacks. Used only occasionally in today's literature.

Cyber Crime – This is any crime that involves a computer and/or a network in its commission. A cyber crime differs from a computer crime in that many cyber crimes can be committed both with and without a computer. Ex: the distribution of child pornography.

Cyber Space – This is a term coined by William Gibson in his 1984 book *Neuromancer*, and is used to describe the virtual world one enters when they go on the Internet.

Cyber Trail – This refers to the trail of digital evidence left behind by a victim or a perpetrator that assists law enforcement in solving a case.

Data Manipulation – This is the term describing the adding, deleting, or rearranging of data in a computer file that has been compromised by a hacker. When a hacker breaks into a system he will manipulate the data to disguise his attack.

DCS1000 – This is the new name for FBI's Carnivore; Carnivore is an e-mail capture program that is installed on an ISP's server. The program scans the subject line and the header information of e-mail and then copies the e-mail if it contains certain names or phrases. The name was changed because many felt Carnivore brought up negative images of an evil meat-eating program.

DEFCON – This is the annual hacker convention held in Las Vegas, Nevada. This is where most hacking groups reveal their latest software and security exploits. Professionals in the security industry and federal law enforcement also attend in order to convince hackers to go straight and to learn how to protect against the exploits revealed.

DOD Wipe Standard – Department of Defense – This is the level of security used by the Department of Defense when it erases data from a hard drive, usually consisting of a series of 7 or more wipes of the hard drive. Since data is not removed from the hard drive when it is deleted, a disk wipe can make the recovery process harder. DOD wipe standard would require government level equipment to recover wiped data.

DOS – Denial of Service – This is a hacker attack in which the victim computer is flooded with data or is hit with a program that consume all of its process control blocks. The goal of this attack is to prevent authorized users from gaining access to the computer or website (web servers are common targets).

Digital Evidence – This refers to evidence stored on any form of digital media, for example evidence stored on a floppy disk or evidence stored on a digital camera.

Dumpster Diving – This refers to the act of rummaging through a dumpster in order to gain information to be used in the commission of a future technology crime. Goal here is to obtain discarded passwords and/or computer manuals that could assist the hacker in infiltrating the computer.

ECPA – Electronic Communications Privacy Act – This is legislation passed in 1986 as a result of growing concern that the Omnibus Crime Control Act of 1968 was not capable of dealing with advances in technology. Main effect on computers is that this law controls what information an ISP can give out with a subpoena, a court order, or a warrant.

E5 – This is the hexadecimal number that replaces the first two letters of a file name to indicate to the operating system that the space is no longer in use and that new information can be saved to that area of the hard drive.

E-Mail – This is electronic mail that uses the Internet as a means of transmitting communications between individuals.

Encryption – This term refers to the mathematical technique for scrambling data so that others cannot read the information without having a password.

ESN – Electronic Serial Number – This is the electronic identification number assigned to a cell phone, the number is used to identify the owner of the phone when a call is made.

Ethernet – This is the early local area network technology developed by Xerox Corporation in the 1970s. The technology was developed so that Xerox could maximize its use of its computers by sharing applications, files, and printers.

Exploits – This is the term used to describe a security vulnerability that has been exposed and exploited by a hacker. Some hackers post their exploits on hacker websites as a means of impressing others and also providing details for newbies to try.

Grooming – This is the process a pedophile will go through in desensitizing a child to sexual contact in order that they may eventually make contact with the child with the intention of having a sexual relationship with the child.

Hacker – This is an individual who gains unauthorized access to another's computer using a combination of computer programming skills and software. Originally this term was used to describe someone who could make computer programs do more than they were originally designed to do. The term became associated with criminals because of the media's coverage of several early computer crimes.

Hex editor – This is a software program that allows the user to examine a disk one bit at a time. One bit is equal to one character.

High Technology Crime – This term is used to describe a crime that is committed with the assistance of a highly technological electronic device. The two most common categories are computer crimes and cyber crimes.

Imaging – This is the term used to describe the forensic copying of a computer's hard drive. It is called an image instead of a copy because the imaged hard drive has all of the same information, including the data in slack space, as the original hard drive did. This is the equivalent of a bit copy of a hard drive.

Identity Theft – This is the term used to describe the theft of someone's personal information. There are two types of identity theft: 1) Physical Identity Theft – this is the theft of someone's actual identity; I.D. thief will assume the victim's life and 2) Financial Identity Theft – here the I.D. thief will assume the victim's credit life.

Internet – This is a worldwide network that consists of electronic mail, ftp services, and the World Wide Web. The Internet has been around for decades, but was released to the public in 1992.

IP Address – Internet Protocol Address This is the number assigned to every computer that accesses the Internet; the number is generally designated as xx.xx.xx.xx and can be used by law enforcement to identify who sent an e-mail or visited a given website.

IP Spoofing – This is a hacking technique where a computer user will make their computer appear to be someone's computer by forging the Internet Protocol Address assigned to computers when a user signs on to the Internet.

IRC – Internet Relay Chat – This is a collection of various channels and chat rooms that allows users to conduct synchronous messaging. IRC channels are usually described by #name of chat room; Ex: #hackz.

ISP –Internet Service Provider - This is the organization through which other users gain access to the Internet. An easy analogy would be to consider an ISP the access ramp to the information super highway. The term organization is used because an ISP can be a public, commercial business or it may be a governmental entity such as a university.

Key Logger – This is the traditional term used to describe computer software that was capable of recording, storing and then e-mailing a list of every keystroke entered into the computer. Recently, a spy supply company has released a piece of hardware that attaches to the back of a computer where the keyboard normally plugs in, and the keyboard is plugged in to the hardware. This hardware will store several thousand keystrokes that can be easily retrieved at a later date.

Logic Bomb – also known as a time bomb – This a computer attack where a malicious program is installed on a victim's computer and programmed to activate on a certain date, given time, or completion of a particular activity. Once activated these programs will normally overwrite the hard drive erasing all data.

Lolita – This is the term used to define a little girl, usually one who has only recently reached puberty or is prepubescent. The term is believed to come from the novel of the same name. Also used as a keyword for websites that contain sexual images of children.

MIN – Mobile Identification Number – This is the number a cellular phone company uses to determine which phone is making a call and then can begin billing the registered user's account.

MIT – Massachusetts Institute of Technology – This was one of the first universities to offer courses in computer programming. As such, MIT played a large role in the foundation of the ARPANET. It was also students at MIT that coined the term hacker.

Modem – This stands for Modulator/Demodulator and is the device that converts data to signals that can be transmitted via the telephone lines and like wise converts signals received from the phone line into data the computer can read.

Packet – This is data that is transmitted via the Internet after it is broken down into small packets of data in order that the information can be transmitted faster and takes full advantage of all network resources.

Packet Sniffer – This software reads the identifying information for every packet of information that a computer sends or receives. The sniffer can be programmed to copy any packets that contain preset types of information.

PATRIOT ACT – Also USA PATRIOT ACT – Uniting and Strengthening America by Providing Appropriate Tools Required to Investigate and Obstruct Terrorism Act – This is the final anti-terrorism act that was recently passed through Congress after the events of September 11, 2001. The actual act is over 300 pages in length and provides for broader police powers to investigate crimes that could be associated with acts of terrorism.

PBX – Public Branch Exchange – This is the computer that a phone company uses in order to control the transfer of telephone calls.

Phreak Box – This is an electrical device that manipulates the telephone system into doing a variety of different functions. There are reportedly over 100 different types of phreak boxes, each distinguishable by color.

Phreaking – This is the act of stealing telecommunication services. This act is normally committed through the use of a telephone, thereby leading to the spelling that begins with "ph" instead of the "f" that the pronunciation would lead one to believe.

Piggybacking – This refers to the act of using another individual's authorized access for another to gain unauthorized access. A common technique is to wait outside the restricted area and when someone enters, the perpetrator will follow the user into the area.

Port – These are the areas on a computer where data enters and exits the computer. Some programs have set ports that are used to access the files, for example port 80 is the http port and is the port that data is received from web pages on.

Port Scanner – This is a computer program that will scan the Internet for IP Addresses that have open ports. An open port is necessary for a computer to receive data. There are manuals written for hackers detailing which security vulnerability programs to run on which open ports.

SATAN – Systems Administrators Tool for Analyzing Networks – This is a network analysis tool that scans a network and reports on any known security weaknesses. The program is rather old and it is the belief of many that it is outdated.

Search Engine – These are web sites that search the Internet for keywords the user has entered. The key words are stored in the header information of all web pages on the Internet and cannot be seen in the normal browser.

Shoulder Surfing – This term refers to the art of looking over a victim's shoulder as they enter in some sort of secret code or personal information. This technique is used quite often by identity thieves to obtain social security numbers and personal information as some one writes out a check.

Slack Space – This is the area of space left over when a new file is written onto the clusters. If a file is 20kb in size then the file will take up 1 entire 16kb cluster and then 4kb of another cluster. The remaining 12kb is what is known as slack space. While not viewable under normal circumstances, there is software that allows for a user to examine the remnants of files in slack space.

Social Engineering – This is the term used to describe activities where a legitimate user of a computer system is tricked into revealing his or her login and password. There are a variety of techniques for this, but most are fairly similar; a perpetrator will pretend to be an authorized user having trouble and needs the victim to assist them in accessing the system.

Spam – This is unsolicited bulk e-mail that is received by a user. The term spam came from an old Monty Python skit.

Trace Route – This is a program that allows a user to see exactly where a request for information travels along the Internet, the result listing will show every server that the request travels through. There are new versions for law enforcement that actually depict the travel in map form so that law enforcement can trace where a suspect's IP address is operating.

Trojan Horse – This is a malicious program that hides itself within another program. Once activated the program can install itself onto the victim's computer and begin running its own functions. The most common function is that a Trojan horse program will allow a remote user to gain access to the victim's computer.

UNIX – This is an early operating system developed by Bell Labs. This operating system is very reliable and is normally run on larger computers such as a business' mainframe. A home version was released in the 1990s called Linux.

URL – Universal Resource Locator – This is the required information that a web browser (Netscape, Internet Explorer, etc.) needs to access a web page. Another way of describing this would be to call it the actual Internet address of a website.

Virus – This is a malicious code that installs itself on a victim's computer and then performs one of several different functions. Many viruses are designed to destroy information. Viruses are transferred from user to user along with valid executable file commands.

War Dialer – This is a computer program that dials a predetermined list of phone numbers in an attempt to determine whether there is a computer on the other end of the phone line that is set to receive phone calls from other computers. This program was made famous in the 1980s with the movie WarGames.

Warez – This is the hacker slang term for software that has had its copyright protection cracked. Author Wallace Wang (1998) claims that this term is used most often with cracked video games.

Web Spoofing – This is when an Internet user's request for one web page is intercepted and redirected to a false website in order to defraud the user. An example would be the individual attempting to get to www.whatever.com may accidentally type in www.whateve.com and get a website that appears to be the actual website. When a user attempts to make a purchase on the website their credit card numbers are submitted to the fake site.

World Wide Web – This is a system of Internet servers that support specially formatted documents. The documents are formatted in a script called hypertext markup language that supports links to other documents, as well as graphics, audio, and video files. This means you can jump from one document to another simply by clicking on links.

Worm – This program replicates itself from computer to computer. A worm, unlike a virus, does not always cause harm to a computer system, but instead wreaks havoc by slowing down the Internet or the computer in the course of copying itself and transmitting the new copies.

APPENDIX B

Text of Section 2703 (c)(1) of the Electronics Communications Privacy Act of 1986

Section 2703(c)(1) of the ECPA provides:
(1) A governmental entity may require a provider of electronic communication service or remote computing service to disclose a record or other information pertaining to a subscriber to or customer of such service (not including the contents of communications) only when the governmental entity--
    (A) obtains a warrant issued using the procedures described in the Federal Rules of Criminal Procedure by a court with jurisdiction over the offense under investigation or equivalent State warrant;
    (B) obtains a court order for such disclosure under subsection (d) of this section;
    (C) has the consent of the subscriber or customer to such disclosure; or
    (D) submits a formal written request relevant to a law enforcement investigation concerning telemarketing fraud for the name, address, and place of business of a subscriber or customer of such provider, which subscriber or customer is engaged in telemarketing (as such term is defined in section 2325 of this title); or
    (E) seeks information under paragraph (2).

Further, subsection (d) that is referred to in section (B) above states:

(d) Requirements for court order.--A court order for disclosure under subsection (b) or (c) may be issued by any court that is a court of competent jurisdiction described in section 3127(2)(A) and shall issue only if the governmental entity offers specific and articulable facts showing that there are reasonable grounds to believe that the contents of a wire or electronic communication, or the records or other information sought, are relevant and material to an ongoing criminal investigation. In the case of a State governmental authority, such a court order shall not issue if prohibited by the law of such State. A court issuing an order pursuant to this section, on a motion made promptly by the service provider, may quash or modify such order, if the information or records requested are unusually voluminous in nature or compliance with such order otherwise would cause an undue burden on such provider.

APPENDIX C

Text of the Computer Fraud and Abuse Act – 18 U.S.C. 1030

Sec. 1030. - Fraud and related activity in connection with computers (a)Whoever –
(1) having knowingly accessed a computer without authorization or exceeding authorized access, and by means of such conduct having obtained information that has been determined by the United States Government pursuant to an Executive order or statute to require protection against unauthorized disclosure for reasons of national defense or foreign relations, or any restricted data, as defined in paragraph y. of section 11 of the Atomic Energy Act of 1954, with reason to believe that such information so obtained could be used to the injury of the United States, or to the advantage of any foreign nation willfully communicates, delivers, transmits, or causes to be communicated, delivered, or transmitted, or attempts to communicate, deliver, transmit or cause to be communicated, delivered, or transmitted the same to any person not entitled to receive it, or willfully retains the same and fails to deliver it to the officer or employee of the United States entitled to receive it;

(2) intentionally accesses a computer without authorization or exceeds authorized access, and thereby obtains –

(A) information contained in a financial record of a financial institution, or of a card issuer as defined in section 1602(n) of title 15, or contained in a file of a consumer reporting agency on a consumer, as such terms are defined in the Fair Credit Reporting Act (15 U.S.C. 1681 et seq.);

(B) information from any department or agency of the United States; or

(C) information from any protected computer if the conduct involved an interstate or foreign communication;

(3) intentionally, without authorization to access any nonpublic computer of a department or agency of the United States, accesses such a computer of that department or agency that is exclusively for the use of the Government of the United States or, in the case of a computer not exclusively for such use, is used by or for the Government of the United States and such conduct affects that use by or for the Government of the United States;

(4) knowingly and with intent to defraud, accesses a protected computer without authorization, or exceeds authorized access, and by means of such conduct furthers the intended fraud and obtains anything of value, unless the object of the fraud and the thing obtained consists only of the use of the computer and the value of such use is not more than $5,000 in any 1-year period;

(5)(A) knowingly causes the transmission of a program, information, code, or command, and as a result of such conduct, intentionally causes damage without authorization, to a protected computer;
(B) intentionally accesses a protected computer without authorization, and as a result of such conduct, recklessly causes damage; or
(C) intentionally accesses a protected computer without authorization, and as a result of such conduct, causes damage;

(6) knowingly and with intent to defraud traffics (as defined in section 1029) in any password or similar information through which a computer may be accessed without authorization, if –
(A) such trafficking affects interstate or foreign commerce; or
(B) such computer is used by or for the Government of the United States; [1] "or".

(7) with intent to extort from any person, firm, association, educational institution, financial institution, government entity, or other legal entity, any money or other thing of value, transmits in interstate or foreign commerce any communication containing any threat to cause damage to a protected computer; shall be punished as provided in subsection (c) of this section.
(b) Whoever attempts to commit an offense under subsection (a) of this section shall be punished as provided in subsection (c) of this section.
(c) The punishment for an offense under subsection (a) or (b) of this section is –

(1) (A) a fine under this title or imprisonment for not more than ten years, or both, in the case of an offense under subsection (a)(1) of this section which does not occur after a conviction for another offense under this section, or an attempt to commit an offense punishable under this subparagraph; and

(B) a fine under this title or imprisonment for not more than twenty years, or both, in the case of an offense under subsection (a)(1) of this section which occurs after a conviction for another offense under this section, or an attempt to commit an offense punishable under this subparagraph;

(2) (A) a fine under this title or imprisonment for not more than one year, or both, in the case of an offense under subsection (a)(2), (a)(3), (a)(5)(C), or (a)(6) of this section which does not occur after a conviction for another offense under this section, or an attempt to commit an offense punishable under this subparagraph; and [2]

(B) a fine under this title or imprisonment for not more than 5 years, or both, in the case of an offense under subsection (a)(2), if –

(i) the offense was committed for purposes of commercial advantage or private financial gain;
(ii) the offense was committed in furtherance of any criminal or tortious act in violation of the Constitution or laws of the United States or of any State; or
(iii) the value of the information obtained exceeds $5,000; [3] So in original. Probably should be followed by "and".

(C) a fine under this title or imprisonment for not more than ten years, or both, in the case of an offense under subsection (a)(2), (a)(3) or (a)(6) of this section which occurs after a conviction for another offense under this section, or an attempt to commit an offense punishable under this subparagraph; and

(3) (A) a fine under this title or imprisonment for not more than five years, or both, in the case of an offense under subsection (a)(4), (a)(5)(A), (a)(5)(B), or (a)(7) of this section which does not occur after a conviction for another offense under this section, or an attempt to commit an offense punishable under this subparagraph; and
(B) a fine under this title or imprisonment for not more than ten years, or both, in the case of an offense under subsection (a)(4), (a)(5)(A), (a)(5)(B), (a)(5)(C), or (a)(7) of this section which occurs after a conviction for another offense under this section, or an attempt to commit an offense punishable under this subparagraph; and [4]

(d) The United States Secret Service shall, in addition to any other agency having such authority, have the authority to investigate offenses under subsections (a)(2)(A), (a)(2)(B), (a)(3), (a)(4), (a)(5), and (a)(6) of this section. Such authority of the United States Secret Service shall be exercised in accordance with an agreement which shall be entered into by the Secretary of the Treasury and the Attorney General.

(e) As used in this section –
(1) the term "computer" means an electronic, magnetic, optical, electrochemical, or other high speed data processing device performing logical, arithmetic, or storage functions, and includes any data storage facility or communications facility directly related to or operating in conjunction with such device, but such

term does not include an automated typewriter or typesetter, a portable hand held calculator, or other similar device;

(2) the term "protected computer" means a computer - **(A)** exclusively for the use of a financial institution or the United States Government, or, in the case of a computer not exclusively for such use, used by or for a financial institution or the United States Government and the conduct constituting the offense affects that use by or for the financial institution or the Government; or **(B)** which is used in interstate or foreign commerce or communication; **(3)** the term "State" includes the District of Columbia, the Commonwealth of Puerto Rico, and any other commonwealth, possession or territory of the United States;

(4) the term "financial institution" means - **(A)** an institution, with deposits insured by the Federal Deposit Insurance Corporation;
(B) the Federal Reserve or a member of the Federal Reserve including any Federal Reserve Bank;
(C) a credit union with accounts insured by the National Credit Union Administration;
(D) a member of the Federal home loan bank system and any home loan bank;
(E) any institution of the Farm Credit System under the Farm Credit Act of 1971;
(F) a broker-dealer registered with the Securities and Exchange Commission pursuant to section 15 of the Securities Exchange Act of 1934;
(G) the Securities Investor Protection Corporation;
(H) a branch or agency of a foreign bank (as such terms are defined in paragraphs (1) and (3) of section 1(b) of the International Banking Act of 1978); and
(I) an organization operating under section 25 or section 25(a) [5] of the Federal Reserve Act.

(FOOTNOTE 6) [6] So in original. The period probably should be a semicolon.

(5) the term "financial record" means information derived from any record held by a financial institution pertaining to a customer's relationship with the financial institution;

(6) the term "exceeds authorized access" means to access a computer with authorization and to use such access to obtain or alter information in the computer that the accesser is not entitled so to obtain or alter;

(7) the term "department of the United States" means the legislative or judicial branch of the Government or one of the executive departments enumerated in section 101 of title 5; and [7]

(8) the term "damage" means any impairment to the integrity or availability of data, a program, a system, or information, that

(A) causes loss aggregating at least $5,000 in value during any 1-year period to one or more individuals;

(B) modifies or impairs, or potentially modifies or impairs, the medical examination, diagnosis, treatment, or care of one or more individuals;

(C) causes physical injury to any person; or

(D) threatens public health or safety; and

(9) the term "government entity" includes the Government of the United States, any State or political subdivision of the United States, any foreign country, and any state, province, municipality, or other political subdivision of a foreign country.

(f) This section does not prohibit any lawfully authorized investigative, protective, or intelligence activity of a law enforcement agency of the United

States, a State, or a political subdivision of a State, or of an intelligence agency of the United States.

(g) Any person who suffers damage or loss by reason of a violation of this section may maintain a civil action against the violator to obtain compensatory damages and injunctive relief or other equitable relief. Damages for violations involving damage as defined in subsection (e)(8)(A) are limited to economic damages. No action may be brought under this subsection unless such action is begun within 2 years of the date of the act complained of or the date of the discovery of the damage.

(h) The Attorney General and the Secretary of the Treasury shall report to the Congress annually, during the first 3 years following the date of the enactment of this subsection, concerning investigations and prosecutions under subsection (a)(5).

INDEX

.avi, 35
.jpeg, 35
.mp3, 44
.mpeg, 35

A

Advanced Research Projects Agency Network, 22
Alana Shears v. Epson America Inc., 111
America Online, 60
Anti-Terrorism Act, 28
ARPANET. *See* Advanced Research Projects Agency Network
articulable fact court order, 108
Ashcroft v. Free Speech Coalition, 57

B

BBSes. *See* Bulletin Board Services
Bearshare, 45
blue box, 30
Boyd v. United States, 115
bulletin board services, 41
Bumper v. North Carolina, 102

C

Cales v. Howell, 134
Capt'n Crunch. *See John Draper*
Carnivore. *See* DCS1000
CD-ROM, 35
chain of custody form, 92
child pornography, 5, 18, 33
Chimel v. California, 99
cluster, 67
computer crime, 2, 18
Computer Fraud and Abuse Act of 1986, 25
Cornell Commission, 25
court order, 112
crackers, 22
cracking. *See* hacking
credit fraud, 5
credit identity theft, 46
cyber crime, 1, 34
cyber stalking, 33
cyber trail, 66
cyberspace, 11

D

Daubert v. Merrill Dow Pharmaceuticals, 72
Davis v. State, 118
DCS1000, 109
digital child pornography, 6, 35
digital crime scene, 14, 86, 96
digital evidence, 66, 94
Donn B. Parker, 8
dumpster diving, 47
DVD-ROMs, 92

E

E5, 67
Electronic Communications Privacy Act of 1986, 107
Electronic Freedom Foundation, 61
E-mail, 43
embezzlement, 6
EnCase, 72
encryption, 6

F

false-friend doctrine, 108
Fourth Amendment, 11, 75
Frye v. United States, 72

G

good faith clause, 81
grooming, 36

grooming via e-mail, 43
Guidance Software, 72

H

hack, 20
hacker, 20
Hacking, 3, 17, *See* cracking
hash value, 71
Helena, 41
Hel-Lo. *See* Helena
high tech crime. *See* high technology crime
High technology crime, 3
honey pot, 55

I

Identity theft
  types, 5, 46
Illinois v. Lafayette, 124
Illinois v. McArthur, 123
Illinois v. Rodriguez, 119
image, 79
intellectual property theft, 6
IP address, 55

J

Jimenez v. State, 118
John Draper, 29
Johnson v. United States, 97

K

Kevin Mitnick, 26, 143
Kevin Poulsen, 4, 32, 113, 143
kit hard drive, 94

L

Limewire, 45
Linux, 90
Lolita, 41
Love Bug virus, 6

M

Massachusetts Institute of Technology, 20
Matter of Search Warrant for K-Sports Imports, Inc., 77
MD5. *See* hash value
Music City Morpheus, 45

N

Napster, 12, 44
narcotics trafficking, 18
New Jersey v. T.L.O., 132
no-knock warrant, 86

O

O'Connor v. Ortega, 136, 137
Ohio v. Robinette, 103
Operation Blue Ridge Thunder, 58
Operation Innocent Images, 56

P

P2P networking. *See* peer-to-peer networking
Parkhurst v. Trapp, 98
Pedophilia, 34
Peer-to-peer networking, 44
phreak, 29
phreaking, 28
physical identity theft, 5, 48
Preston v. United States, 98
Privlic, 107

R

RAM. *See* Random Access Memory
Random Access Memory, 89
Robert Morris, 24

Index

S

Schneckloth v. Bustamonte, 115
search warrant, 75
Search Warrant Team, 82
Secret Service, 85
shoulder-surfing, 47
slack space, 68
State v. Hammonds, 117
steganography, 6
Steve Jobs, 30, 118
Stoner v. California, 103
subpoena, 111

T

Tatsuo Shimomura, 26
Telecommunications fraud. See phreaking
terrorism, 28
theft of bandwidth, 6
totality of the circumstances test, 103
Traceroute, 55

U

United States v. Hunter, 77
United States v. Alfonso, 121
United States v. Ball, 100
United States v. Barth, 105, 130
United States v. Bizier, 99
United States v. Blas, 105, 116
United States v. Burns, 97
United States v. Carey, 78, 116, 127
United States v. Charbonneau, 107
United States v. David, 106, 121
United States v. Durham, 119
United States v. Elliot, 104
United States v. Gray, 78, 129
United States v. Haddad, 113
United States v. Hall, 130
United States v. Hambrick, 108
United States v. Lyons, 106

United States v. Matlock, 119
United States v. Maxwell, 127
United States v. Moorehead, 123
United States v. Ortiz, 122
United States v. Poulsen, 113
United States v. Rahme, 114
United States v. Ramsey, 138
United States v. Reed, 121
United States v. Reyes, 125
United States v. Roberts, 139
United States v. Robinson, 124
United States v. Romero-Garcia, 122
United States v. Ross, 104
United States v. Scheer, 138
United States v. Smith, 119
United States v. Tank, 124
United States v. Tucker, 42
United States v. Upham, 77
United States v. Villarreal, 128
UNIX, 90
USA PATRIOT Act, 28, 59

V

vigilante hacker groups, 53
Virtual identity theft, 47
VisualRoute, 55

W

Walter v. United States, 130
Warden v. Hayden, 100
warrantless search
    consent, 101
    exigent circumstances, 99, 120
    incident to a lawful arrest, 98
    plain view, 101
    school searches, 132
    third-party consent, 103
warrantless search doctrine, 98
West Virginia v. Joseph T., 133
Windows Operating System, 89
Windows X, 90
WinMx, 45
World Wide Web, 20